ROY BENNETT

Bucklers Mead School, Yeovil

Enjoying music

BOOK 1

LONGMAN

How an orchestra is laid out.

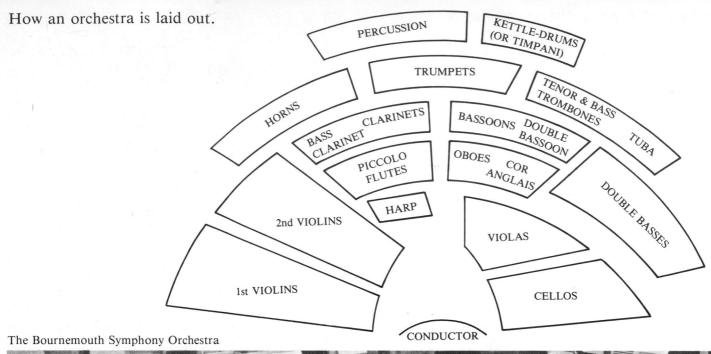

PERCUSSION

KETTLE-DRUMS (OR TIMPANI)

TRUMPETS

TENOR & BASS TROMBONES

HORNS

CLARINETS

BASS CLARINET

BASSOONS

DOUBLE BASSOON

TUBA

PICCOLO FLUTES

OBOES COR ANGLAIS

2nd VIOLINS

HARP

DOUBLE BASSES

VIOLAS

1st VIOLINS

CELLOS

CONDUCTOR

The Bournemouth Symphony Orchestra

Bedřich Smetana CZECHOSLOVAKIA (BOHEMIA) 1824-1884

Vltava

from Má Vlast (My Country)

Czechoslovakia, now a Communist State, was formed in 1918 by joining together the Czechs of the western part of the country, known as the Kingdom of Bohemia, with the Slovaks of the eastern part.

Before 1918, the country had been part of the Austrian Empire, and the Austrians had treated the Czechs very harshly. At one time, the performance of plays and operas in the Czech language was forbidden. But the Austrians began to fear a Czech revolution and so, in the 1860's, they allowed a theatre to be built in Prague where the Czechs might perform plays and operas in their own language. The first Musical Director of this National Theatre was Bedřich Smetana. Czech composers naturally wanted to express their love for their own country. Operas were written based upon national legends; orchestral pieces called 'tone poems' — music which tells a story, or paints a picture in sound — were composed, often using folk tunes and the lively rhythms of Czech dances such as the Polka. Smetana himself wrote a set of six orchestral tone poems which he called *Má Vlast* ('My Country'). The second of these is called *Vltava*, and tells the story of a Czech river from its source until it reaches the city of Prague.

Smetana could play the violin at the age of four, and the piano when he was six. But his father, who was a wealthy brewer, at first did not want his son to become a musician. Later, Smetana studied at Prague and became the first composer to write music using Czech folk tunes and dance rhythms. He composed several operas about Czech life which he conducted at the National Theatre in Prague.

It was about the time when he was composing the first of the six pieces called 'My Country' that he first started to go deaf. At first, he noticed a high-pitched whistling note in his ears, and often heard sounds like rushing water. Then everything he heard became distorted. He had to give up conducting the orchestra. In 1847 he suddenly became totally deaf, but he still went on writing music. He wrote 'Vltava' without hearing a single note of the music.

In 1882, two years before Smetana died, 'My Country' was performed in Prague. After each piece there was great applause, people waved their hats and handkerchiefs in the air and shouted Smetana's name. The composer, stone deaf, stood in the middle of them all, rather bewildered but, as a friend said, 'happy in the knowledge that he had given happiness to others . . .'.

In the end, his memory began to fail him, and his speech was affected. He died in an asylum at the age of 60.

Smetana headed his music with a description of the course of the River Vltava. This is how it begins: 'Ze dvou praménků vzniká, o kameny zvoní a ve slunci se kmitá, mohutní, na její březích ozývá se honba a později venkovsky tánec.' (The river springs from two sources, splashing gaily over the rocks and glistening in the sunshine. As it broadens, the banks re-echo with the sound of hunting-horns and country dances.)

The River Vltava and Prague as it appeared in Smetana's time.

Points to listen for

1. The source of the River Vltava. In high forest country, two springs gush forth — one warm and racing, the other cool and tranquil (A). The music becomes more flowing as the two streams join to make one: *pizzicato* (plucked) strings and harp splashes.

2. The river's flowing theme, played on violins and oboe (B).

3. A colourful hunting scene in the forest: 4 horns (C).

4. The Vltava flows past a village where a wedding feast is taking place. The rhythm changes and we hear a polka danced on the banks by peasants in gay costumes: strings and clarinets (D).

5. Night falls, and silvery *russalki* (Czech water-nymphs) dance and bathe in the moonlight: high shimmering muted strings, woodwind and harp (E).

6. The river approaches the turbulent St. John Rapids. Swirling rhythms, rumbling basses, woodwind shrieks, and vivid cymbals suggest the crashing of spray upon the rocks. (Remember that Smetana was stone deaf when he wrote this music, and never heard a single note of it except in his imagination.)

7. We emerge from the rapids and the Vltava, now a broad and mighty river, flows majestically on towards the city of Prague, its song now in the triumphant major key. It passes beneath the famous bridge decorated with statues of men famous in Bohemian history, including St. Wenceslas of the Christmas carol. The river then flows away into the distance (but the music ends with two loud chords).

5

Camille Saint-Saëns: FRANCE 1835-1921

Danse Macabre

Saint-Saëns made his first public appearance in Paris at the age of nine, playing the piano for a famous Belgian violinist. Later on, he became an organist, playing at the Madeleine, a famous church in Paris, for 20 years. But he was really known as a composer and a brilliant pianist. On his 85th birthday he gave a concert, playing the piano part in one of his concertos.

Unlike some composers, Saint-Saëns found writing music very easy. In fact, people said he could write down a new piece while carrying on a witty conversation with visitors at the same time.

He was particularly interested in animals and wrote a book called 'Observations of a Friend of Animals'. One of his most famous compositions is called *Carnival of Animals* — fourteen short pieces for two pianos and a small group of instruments. They describe various 'creatures', including an elephant, tortoises, a swan, fossils — and pianists! It was a kind of musical joke, written to amuse his closest friends. Perhaps for this reason Saint-Saëns would not let the music be performed in public during his lifetime.

A mediaeval woodcut showing the Dance of Death.

The xylophone
A xylophone has bars of hard wood laid out rather like the arrangement of black and white keys on a piano. Each wooden bar is tuned to a certain note. The player hits the bars with wooden sticks, or occasionally, with hard rubber beaters if a softer tone is required. (A glockenspiel is a similar instrument, except that the bars are made of metal).

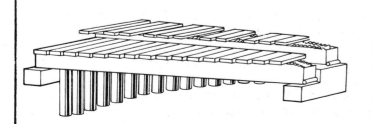

The violin
The violin is really a hollow box with the upper side (or belly) made of pine, and the rest of sycamore. The 4 strings (of gut, or metal, or both) are attached at one end to the tail-piece and at the other to the tuning-pegs. They are stretched across the bridge, which supports them and prevents them from touching the body of the instrument. The strings are tuned to the notes G D A E.

To produce the sound, the violinist draws the bow across the strings. To obtain different notes he must shorten the strings. He does this by pressing a string against the finger-board with his finger. The strings can then only vibrate along the length from the bridge to the player's finger. The shorter the string, the higher the note.

Instead of using the bow, the player can pluck the strings rather like a guitar. This is called *pizzicato*.

Another well-known piece by Saint-Saëns is *Danse Macabre* — an orchestral piece based upon a poem by the French writer, Henri Cazalis. The music describes the gruesome happenings in the churchyard of a small French village on Hallowe'en.

Danse Macabre was once performed in the Catacombs of Paris!

Zig-a-zig-a-zig — it's the rhythm of Death!
His heels tap the tomb-stones as he tunes his violin.
Death at midnight, playing a dance-tune —
Zig-a-zig-a-zig on his violin.
The winter wind whistles and the night is dark;
The winter wind whistles and the lime-trees moan.
Weird, white skeletons streak across the shadows;
Running and leaping, wrapped in their shrouds.
Zig-a-zig-a-zig — the dance grows even wilder;
You can hear the eerie clatter of the dancers' bones . . .
But wait! Suddenly, they all stop dancing!
They scatter . . . they vanish — for the cock has crowed!

This is how Cazalis' poem begins in French:

Zig et zig et zig, la Mort en cadence
Frappant une tombe avec son talon,
La Mort à minuit joue un air de danse
Zig et zig et zig, sur son violon.

Points to listen for

1. The twelve soft chimes of the witching hour of midnight are heard on harp and French horn (A).

2. The mysterious cloaked figure of Death stealthily appears. He drums his heels upon the tombstones (B) and then tunes his violin (C), urging the skeletons to rise from their graves.

3. They begin to dance, stealthily at first, to a waltz tune heard first on the flute, then on the violins (D).

4. Then Death plays the main waltz tune upon his violin (E).

5. Tune F on oboe and bassoon, echoed by Death's violin. Later, we hear the first phrase of this tune on the violin and the second on the xylophone, imitating the eerie clatter of the dancers' bones. (It is this tune which Saint-Saëns used later, also on the xylophone but with slightly changed rhythm, to represent 'Fossils' in *Carnival of Animals*.)

6. The pace of the waltz becomes more and more frantic. The strings suggest the wind rustling through the grave-yard trees. At the climax of the music the violins play Tune D while, at the same time, Tune E is heard on the trombones.

7. Then, after this dramatic impression of sound and movement, there is a sudden silence — as the oboe signifies cock-crow and the first light of dawn.

8. Immediately, the skeletons disappear into their graves. There is a reminder of Death's melancholy violin; then he, too, disappears . . .

7

Modeste Mussorgsky RUSSIA 1839-1881

A Night on the Bare Mountain

Arranged by Rimsky-Korsakov

In the 1860's in St. Petersburg, the Russian composer Balakirev gave four other amateur musicians lessons in composition. The group became known as 'The Mighty Handful', or simply 'The Russian Five'.

Their aim was to write music which was truly Russian in flavour, and not influenced by the great German composers of the time. All five musicians had once followed other careers. Balakirev (1), was once a mathematician; Rimsky-Korsakov (2), a sailor; Borodin (3), a chemist; Cui (4), a soldier; Mussorgsky (5), also a soldier.

1   2   3   4

5

Mussorgsky was the son of a rich Russian landowner. His grandfather had been an officer in the Imperial Guards and so, when Mussorgsky left school, he was sent to a military academy. But he had been taught to play the piano by his mother, and he went on having piano lessons at the academy. He became a brilliant pianist and made friends with many Russian musicians, including the composer Balakirev, who later gave him lessons in composition. Mussorgsky soon decided to give up his career as a soldier and to become a composer instead. He found it difficult to earn enough money through music and was forced to take a job in a government office. After the death of his mother, whom he had always loved deeply, he began to drink heavily — a problem he never really overcame for the rest of his life.

Some of Mussorgsky's music was performed, but it was often misunderstood, since it seemed so brutal and stark. He left several pieces unfinished, and his friend Rimsky-Korsakov completed some of them, and tried to 'correct' the roughness in the orchestral writing. But it is this very brashness of instrumental colouring which appeals to many listeners today.

'As far as talent is concerned, Mussorgsky is the most important of them all, but he never seeks perfection. He is convinced of his own genius. He seems to be proud of his ignorance and writes whatever occurs to him on the spur of the moment. But truly his absolutely original talent is shown everywhere in his music. He speaks a new language.'

(Tchaikovsky)

Mussorgsky's bouts of drunkenness became more frequent, and sometimes he would disappear for weeks at a time. He lost his government job, and died at the age of 42, quite alone, in a charity hospital in St. Petersburg (now Leningrad).

Mussorgsky's music gives a vivid impression of a Witches' Sabbath, which in Russian folklore takes place on Midsummer's Eve on Bare Mountain, near Kiev in southern Russia. It is on this night that demons and witches meet to dance wildly and celebrate their Sabbath. Mussorgsky actually wrote the music on Midsummer's Eve, 1867.

The peasants who live near Bare Mountain still place nettles on thresholds and window-sills to ward off witches and evil spirits.

trombone

piccolo

oboe

Points to listen for

1. Soft rustling strings, with shrill warnings from oboes and bassoon (A). Trombones above the roll of a bass drum announce the emergence of spirits (B). Crashing chords suggest vivid flashes of lightning as the Devil himself appears. Then this section is repeated a semi-tone higher.

2. A wild dance begins on woodwind and strings (C).

3. A pause, followed by theme D as witches arrive to perform a Black Mass in homage to the Devil. Above the confusion the shrill voice of the piccolo is often heard, while the varied percussion section and blazing brass emphasise the dramatic contrasts of *pp* and *ff* (very soft and very loud).

4. A return to the opening music (A and B) and the wild dance (C).

5. Again, the pause, followed by theme D.

6. Then there is a thunderous crash on the tam-tam (a large gong) and a sudden dramatic silence from which the distant sound of church-bells emerges.

7. The strings herald the dawn — peace and light after darkness and confusion. The serene pastoral melody of the *coda* (E) suggests a shepherd playing his pipe on the mountainside as day breaks on the now peaceful scene.

'The Witch made her own arrangements to attend the Sabbath; she smeared herself with flying ointment . . . and rode on a forked stick or broom through the air. Alternatively, she might receive from the Devil a goat, ram, or dog for this purpose. Sabbaths were held in various places — crossroads, woods, wild fields, or even churches . . .'
(from *A Dictionary of Witchcraft*)

tam-tam

Modeste Mussorgsky RUSSIA 1839-1881

from **Pictures at an exhibition**

Orchestrated by Maurice Ravel FRANCE 1875-1937

When a famous Russian artist, architect and stage designer called Victor Hartmann died in 1873, a memorial exhibition was held showing 400 paintings, drawings and sketches. Mussorgsky, a friend of Hartmann's, attended the exhibition and was inspired by his visit to write ten piano pieces, each describing one of the exhibits. The work—his only large work for the piano—was composed in a single month: June, 1874.

Although Mussorgsky was a brilliant pianist, his writing for the piano is often rather clumsy. Several musicians have tried to arrange Mussorgsky's piano pieces for full orchestra. Nowadays, *Pictures at an Exhibition* is often heard in Ravel's brilliant version. He had had plenty of practice at this sort of exercise, as he himself often wrote pieces for the piano and orchestrated them later.

Ravel at the piano with some of his friends.

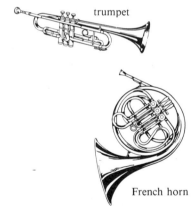

trumpet

French horn

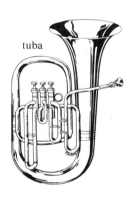

tuba

trombone

Promenade

A short prelude introduces the work, and comes again before some of the pieces, as if to suggest the composer strolling from picture to picture. Ravel uses his orchestra here mainly in sections. A solo trumpet announces the theme (A), answered by the whole brass section — 4 horns, 3 trumpets, 3 trombones and tuba. Notice how the music alternates between 5 and 6 beats to a bar. A five-beat rhythm is characteristic of Russian folk music.

Later, the strings are prominent, followed by two or three bars played chiefly by woodwind. The brass section is important again towards the end.

The Gnome

A deformed, menacing creature who scrabbles and shuffles along, uttering wild shrieks. (Hartmann's original was a design in wood for a nutcracker to be hung on a Christmas tree.) Low strings, clarinets and bassoons first suggest the awkward movements of the Gnome (B), ending with a crash on bass drum and cymbals. Later, listen for:

1. A descending sequence of chords on the woodwind, first with single notes on the xylophone, then repeated by the celesta with eerie *glissando* (sliding) strings.
2. A *fortissimo* (very loud) passage with a theme on muted trumpets (C), ending abruptly with a sharp whip-crack. (The orchestral 'whip' is made of two hinged pieces of wood which are slapped together to give a loud 'crack'.)
3. Buzzing trills and slides on bass clarinet, cellos and double basses leading to:
4. Terrifying discords on muted brass and rattle, suggesting clawed hands ready to attack. Then the Gnome quickly scrabbles away.

The Old Castle

A troubadour sings outside a medieval castle. Two bassoons set the rhythm and the atmosphere, then the haunting melody is played by an alto saxophone (D). Later, muted strings suggest a warm, mysterious summer night. The note G sharp is held right through the piece.

Mutes

Mutes are sometimes used to soften or alter the tone of a musical instrument. Brass instruments use mutes which are cones of wood or metal placed in the bell of the instrument. A trumpet mute does not necessarily make the tone softer, but rather sharper and more metallic. A mute for a string instrument is a small comb-shaped piece of wood with three prongs. When fitted onto the bridge it reduces the vibrations of the strings, giving a softer, more muffled tone.

The saxophone

The saxophone was invented in the 1840's by Adolphe Sax. It is similar in shape to a bass clarinet. Both instruments have a single reed and a similar system of fingering, but as the saxophone is made of brass it belongs to the brass section rather than to the woodwind.

The instrument has a very smooth, mellow tone, ideally suiting it for use in dance bands.

In the Tuileries Gardens

At the time of the French Revolution, the Tuileries was the Royal Palace of the French king. After the palace was destroyed, the gardens became the fashionable spot for Parisians to take a leisurely stroll on sunny afternoons.

Points to listen for

The music is in three sections: *Scherzo, Trio* and *Scherzo,* again. (*Scherzo* is Italian for joke; a *trio* is a contrasting middle section.)

1. Woodwind imitate the voices of children quarrelling and playing games (E). (*Scherzo*).

2. The middle section is more subdued. Strings suggest the meeting and quieter conversation of grown-ups. (*Trio*).

3. Return of the first section. (*Scherzo*).

Bydlo (The Ox-cart)

The melody, played here by the lumbering tuba, is a folk tune sung by a Polish peasant as he drives home his ox-drawn cart (G).

The piece begins quietly, as if the cart is approaching from the distance. You hear the steady tramping of the oxen's feet, and the rumbling of huge wheels. There is a long *crescendo* — the music grows gradually louder as more instruments join in and the cart draws nearer. Then it passes, *fortissimo,* and gradually disappears into the distance in a long *diminuendo* (Italian for 'gradually growing softer').

The tuba

The tuba is the largest instrument in the brass section, and so provides the lowest notes. It has 12 feet of wide tubing, giving the instrument a rich 'fat' tone. The tuba was introduced into the orchestra only about a hundred years ago.

It is rarely given tunes to play. Instead, it adds richness and depth to the bass line. In its higher register, though, it sounds rather like a French horn.

The Hut on Fowls' Legs

Here, Hartmann's picture represented a clock in the form of the cottage of the legendary Russian witch called Baba Yaga. (You can see Hartmann's sketch on the opposite page.)

On top of the hut were two cockerels' heads, and the whole thing stood on fowls' legs, so that Baba Yaga could fly off whenever she wanted.

Mussorgsky's music describes an exciting chase as the witch pursues her victim.

Points to listen for

The music is in three sections.

1. With a pounding, hopping rhythm, emphasised by eruptions on bass drum and kettle-drums, the hut begins to move (H).
2. A triumphant phrase screamed by three trumpets (I).
3. Menacing calls from horns and trombones, as Baba Yaga pursues her victim.
4. *Tremolo* strings (played with short, repeated strokes of the bow) screaming from top to bottom of their register as the hut loses speed and comes to rest.
5. The hopping phrase is still heard in the middle section against a background of trembling woodwind. The music now sounds rather more stealthy, as if the witch were stalking her victim.
6. Sudden explosive chords on *pizzicato* violins, celesta, harp and xylophone.
7. A sudden *fortissimo* chord — the victim is seized!
8. The music of the first section returns as the hut speeds off again at Baba Yaga's command. The music leads without a break into the final 'picture':

The Great Gate of Kiev

This was Hartmann's design for an elaborate Russian Gate with a dome in the shape of a Slavonic helmet. It was to be made of stone and contain a small church. The archway, resting on huge granite pillars, would have been decorated with the Russian eagle. The city council of Kiev had planned to build the Gate to commemorate the escape of Czar Alexander II from attempted assassination on April 4th, 1866. But the gate was never built.

The music gives the impression of an approaching religious procession (J). Twice, woodwind instruments imitate voices singing a Russian hymn (K). Finally, to the tolling of the bells of Kiev, the procession triumphantly enters the Great Gate.

(Opposite page) Hartmann's design for 'Baba Yaga's hut'.

Hartmann's design for the 'Great Gate of Kiev'.

Jean Sibelius FINLAND 1865-1957

FINLANDIA

Finland lies between Sweden and Russia. Until the early 19th century it was ruled by Sweden. After that it became a province of Russia, but it has been an independent country since 1918 — and Finns are fiercely proud of this. About two-thirds of the country is covered by forests of pine, spruce and birch. There are rough outcrops of pinkish granite, and — what you notice most — lakes everywhere. People also refer to Finland as 'green-gold and granite' (green-gold = wealth from timber). It is sometimes called the 'land of 60,000 lakes' because so much of the country is water. In the north and east there are rivers, often with rapids.

'I have always imagined life as a massive block of granite. With will-power for a chisel, you hew the granite until it bears the shape you have sketched out. It is just as important to have your plans ready before you begin to hew the stone as it is to have a sharp chisel. We all have the power to chisel our lives according to our wishes.'   (Sibelius)

A typical Finnish landscape.

Johan Julius Christian Sibelius — he later took the simpler name 'Jean' from an uncle who was a sailor — was born in Tavastehus, about 30 miles north of Finland's capital city, Helsinki. His father, a doctor, wanted him to become a lawyer, but Sibelius tells how, after walking for a whole day and a night in the forests, he made up his mind to become a composer. He wrote mainly songs and orchestral pieces (symphonies and tone poems). *Finlandia* and *The Swan of Tuonela* are tone poems.

Although Sibelius lived to be over 90, he wrote most of his music before he was 60. His pieces portray the sounds and rhythms of the Finnish countryside: forests at night, lonely lakes, sunlight on snow-covered pines, and stormy winds sweeping across the land.

Sibelius had a great love for his country. There is a story that during the 'Winter War' in 1939, when Finland was invaded by the Soviet Union, the composer (then in his seventies) used to take pot shots at Soviet aircraft with his hunting rifle.

Finns think of Sibelius as their national composer, and are extremely proud of him.

At the World Fair in New York in 1939, a cylinder was buried which contained three things: a piece of typical 'pop' music, a march by the American composer Sousa — and *Finlandia*. The cylinder will remain unopened for 5,000 years.

The Sibelius monument in Helsinki.

FINLANDIA

This music was composed in 1899, when Finland was still under Russian rule. A gala evening was held in Helsinki. Six scenes from Finnish life were presented, and Sibelius wrote songs and orchestral music to accompany each one. He called the final piece 'Suomi' — Finnish for Finland, and meaning 'land of fens'. This is the music we now call *Finlandia*.

It was a great success, but aroused the Finns' national feelings so strongly that the Russians banned it. When Sibelius himself conducted it later on, he had to call it *Impromptu*. The Finns look upon the hymn-like melody (Tune D) as a second national anthem.

It is often said that Sibelius used Finnish folk tunes in his music, but he himself said: 'On this point, I can only say that I have never used a theme which I have not created myself.'

Points to listen for

1. A dramatic and menacing beginning on brass and kettle-drums (A), followed by a smoother answering phrase (B) played first by the woodwind, then by the strings.

A quieter phrase, begun by strings then taken over by clarinets.

2. Very loud and rhythmic trumpet-calls alternating with theme A, now played faster.

3. Rumbling kettle-drums and basses introduce the main section of the music: the trumpet-calls again, now with exciting cymbal clashes (C), then a rhythmic theme for strings with triangle.

4. The hymn-like melody (D) played first by woodwind, then by strings.

5. Return of the trumpet-calls, and the music rises to a climax with cymbal clashes off the beat.

At the climax the kettle-drums roar, and the brass crunches in, triumphantly reminding us of the hymn-like theme (D) now much slower.

Jean Sibelius FINLAND 1865-1957

The Swan of Tuonela

The Swan of Tuonela

This is one of the four pieces for orchestra, based upon stories from the Kalevala saga, which Sibelius composed in 1895.

Tuonela is the realm of the dead in Finnish mythology. It is surrounded by a dark river with rapid currents leading to a whirlpool. A majestic black swan glides along the river, singing a melancholy song.

The hero of this legend is a lively dwarf named Lemminkäinen. In order to win his chosen bride, Kylliki, he must perform three tasks — the third being to shoot the Swan of Tuonela.

The river is guarded by a blind and crippled cowherd, who causes a serpent to sting the heart of Lemminkäinen. His body is then torn into pieces and thrown into the river. But Lemminkaïnen's mother rakes out the pieces and by means of her magic powers reassembles the body and restores her son to life.

For this music Sibelius uses an unusual combination of instruments. The strings are divided into many parts — for instance, there are eight groups of violins. The other instruments seem to have been deliberately chosen for their dark tone colours: oboe, bass clarinet, 2 bassoons, 4 horns, 3 trombones, kettle-drums, bass drum and harp. The most important instrument is the *cor anglais,* which plays the melancholy song of the black swan.

The Kalevala

A saga is a long story or collection of legends from northern countries such as Iceland or Finland, telling of the adventures of gods and heroes.

The Finns rediscovered their ancient national saga, the Kalevala, in the 19th century. Since then interest in it has grown. People have written pieces of music and painted pictures about the many legends from the saga, and there is even a kind of jewellery based upon the old designs called Kalevala jewellery.

The saga dates back to the 9th century, and consists of legends handed down through the generations by word of mouth and then finally written down. People used to recite the Kalevala sitting facing each other upon a bench, holding each other's arms and rocking to and fro, as in the stamp.

The cor anglais   The *cor anglais* is really a larger version of the oboe, with a correspondingly lower range of notes. Like the oboe, it has a double reed. This fits into a curved mouthpiece about nine inches long, and gives the instrument a rather dark, melancholy tone colour. The tube is conical, with a bulge at the bell end. The player often supports the instrument by a sling around his neck, rather like a bassoon-player.

The name 'cor anglais' means 'English horn' — which is rather odd since the instrument is not a horn, neither is it English. Some people think the word 'anglais' is really a mis-spelling of the French word 'anglé', meaning 'bent', and possibly referring to the bend in the mouthpiece.

Points to listen for

1. Very soft, mysterious chords on the strings which begin low on basses and cellos, then rise gradually higher and higher. Notice the distinctive tone-colours of the *cor anglais* (A), and solo cello which plays a rising phrase (B).
2. High strings played *tremolo* (with quick, short repeated movements of the bow) offer a mysterious background to the *cor anglais* melody, which gradually becomes more intense.
3. *Pizzicato* violins — then a ripple of harp above the ominous rumble of a bass drum.
4. Soft, rhythmic chords on kettle-drums, horns and trombones, while all the strings except double basses play a rich unison melody.
5. Eerie sounds from the strings: half of them playing normally, the other tapping the strings lightly with the wood of the bow. Still the menacing rumble of the bass drum, while the harp repeats a short phrase over and over again.
6. Then, soft rising chords on the strings as at the very beginning, and a final weaving upwards of the solo cello.

The cello

The cello is roughly twice as big as the violin, but is much deeper front to back. The strings are longer and thicker, so that the notes are lower and the tone full and rich.

The cello used to be gripped between the knees, but towards the end of the last century a spike was added beneath the body of the instrument so that it can be rested on the ground.

The cello's most characteristic sound is smooth and flowing.

The Kalevala (from Runo XIV)

 ärkähattu karjan paimen,
Ukko Pohjolan sokea,
Tuop' on Tuonelan joella,
Pyhän virran pyörtehellä;
Katselevi, käntelevi
Tulevaksi Lemminkäistä.
   Jo päivänä muutamana
Näki lieto Lemminkäisen
Saavaksi, läheneväksi
Tuonne Tuonelan joelle,
Vierehen vihaisen kosken,

This is how the first eleven lines look in the Finnish language.

Märkähattu then, the cowherd,
Pohjola's old sightless greybeard,
There by Tuonela's broad river,
By the sacred river's whirlpool,
Long had lurked and long had waited
There for Lemminkäinen's coming.
And at length one day it happened,
Came the lively Lemminkäinen
Hasting on, and swift approaching
Unto Tuonela's deep river,
To the cataract most terrific,
To the sacred river's whirlpool,
From the waves he sent a serpent,
Like a reed from out the billows;
Through the hero's heart he hurled it,
And through Lemminkäinen's liver.

Through the arm-pit left it smote him,
Through the shoulder right it struck him.
Then the lively Lemminkäinen
Felt himself severely wounded . . .

. . . Floated lively Lemminkäinen,
Down the thundering cataract floated,
Down the rushing streams he floated,
Unto Tuonela's dread dwelling.
Then the bloodstained son of Tuoni
Drew his sword and smote the hero,
With his gleaming blade he hewed him,
While it shed a stream of flashes,
And he hewed him in five fragments,
And in pieces eight he hewed him,
Then in Tuonela's stream cast them . . .

Edvard Grieg NORWAY 1843-1907

Wedding Day at Troldhaugen

Norway is a long, narrow, mountainous country running down the western side of Scandinavia. Nearly three-quarters of the country is rugged and mountainous, and sparsely populated. The people live in the deep valleys between the mountains and around the fjords, as the sea inlets in Norway are called.

'By painting in music Norwegian scenery, the life of the Norwegian people, Norwegian history and Norwegian folk poems, I believe I am really able to achieve something.'
(Edvard Grieg)

Edvard Grieg.

The Hardanger Fjord in Norway.

Grieg's mother could trace her family back to the Vikings, while his father was of Scottish descent. A certain Alexander Greig left Scotland after the Battle of Culloden in 1746 and settled in Bergen, Norway, changing the spelling of his name to the more Norwegian-sounding Grieg.

Like Smetana and Sibelius, Grieg was very interested in the folk music of his own country, and often used Norwegian folk tunes in his music. He was also interested in folklore. His house (in the country near Bergen) was called 'Troldhaugen', meaning 'The Hill of the Trolls'. (A troll is a dwarf in Norwegian folklore.) A great deal of his music was written in a small hut in the grounds of his house. The hut was just large enough for a piano, writing table, chair and fire-place. Here, Grieg could compose his music in peace, looking out over the beautiful Hardanger Fjord to the distant mountains. When Grieg died in 1907, his ashes were buried in a tiny cave carved high in the mountainside above the Hardanger Fjord.

Grieg once took his Piano Concerto to the great Hungarian pianist and composer, Franz Liszt. When Liszt had finished playing it, he jumped up in great excitement and strode about the room, roaring the melody at the top of his voice. Then he dashed back to the piano and played the whole piece through again, orchestral parts included.

Points to listen for

This bright rhythmic music is Grieg's own orchestration of a piano piece he wrote as a wedding anniversary present for his wife, Nina. The music is in *ternary* design—a kind of 'musical sandwich' in three sections: A B A. The first and last sections use the same music; the middle section, (B), forms a contrast (the filling!).

1. A catchy rhythm on low strings introduces a violin melody (A). Repeated by flute with triangle.

2. Brass and snare drum. Then rustling strings lead to a climax excitingly supported by heavy brass.

3. Theme A *fortissimo* (very loud), with brass and cymbals.

4. Middle section, built on a more flowing theme (B). Listen for added notes on the glockenspiel in the repeat.

5. Return of the first section (A).

6. *Coda* (meaning an 'ending' or 'finishing off') based on the opening notes of A.

Grieg's house in Oslo.　　　Grieg's mountain grave.

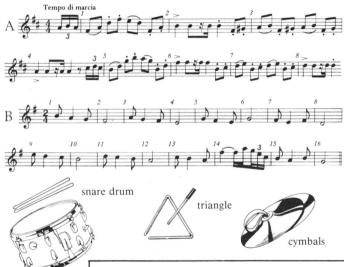

Notice on Grieg's gate at Troldhaugen when he became famous:

> 'EDVARD GRIEG
> REGRETS
> THAT HE CANNOT
> RECEIVE VISITORS
> BEFORE 4 AM'

Facsimile of the first four bars of 'Wedding Day at Troldhaugen'.

Frederick Delius ENGLAND 1862-1934

On hearing the first cuckoo in Spring

Delius was born at Bradford in Yorkshire. His father, who was a rich wool merchant, was determined that he should follow him in the family business. When he found that his son was just as determined to become a composer, he sent him to Florida to manage an orange plantation. But Delius spent more time reading and walking in the woods and by the river, listening to the Negroes making their music, than looking after the estate. Later, he said: 'I loved it (the Negro music), and I started writing music in earnest. In the night, which falls quickly in that part of the world, the sound of Negro voices was enchanting . . . '

When the Norwegian composer Grieg heard some music which Delius had written called 'Florida', he persuaded Delius' father to allow his son to go to Germany to study music at Leipzig.

Eventually, Delius settled down with his wife Jelka, who was a painter, in the tiny French village of Grez-sur-Loing, not far from Paris. The house had a large, beautiful garden leading down to the river, and it was here that Delius wrote all his finest music.

Towards the end of his life, Delius became blind and paralysed. A young musician from Yorkshire named Eric Fenby heard that the composer was no longer able to work. He decided to go to Grez-sur-Loing to see if he could help. And so Delius still continued to compose, by dictating the music to Fenby, who wrote it down.

My works have been the most important events in my life . . .

Frederick Delius

The blind Delius with his wife.

Helping the blind Delius to compose his music proved much more difficult than Fenby had imagined. Here is his account of their first attempt:

'That evening, after supper, Delius surprised me by saying that he had an idea in his mind — a simple little tune — and that he wanted me to take it down.

I took paper and pen and waited eagerly. I had no idea what he would do — whether he would sing, or call out the names of the notes and their varying time-values. What he did was to stagger and confound me so utterly that I did not recover for the rest of that night.

Throwing back his head, he began to drawl in a loud monotone that was little more than the crudest extension of speech . . . This is something like what I heard:

'Ter-te-ter — ter-te-ter — ter-te-ter' — and here he interjected 'Hold it!' and then went on — 'ter-te-te-ter — ter-ter-te-te-te-ter — hold it!' . . .

When he had finished this amazing recital, he turned to me and asked, 'Have you got that? Now sing it!' I was dumbfounded . . . I saw that he evidently heard the tune imaginatively, but was unable to sing it.'

Points to listen for

In this musical description of the freshness and beauty of the countryside awakening in spring, Delius uses a small orchestra consisting of flute, oboe, 2 clarinets, 2 bassoons, 2 horns and strings. Throughout the piece, all the strings except the double basses are divided into two groups.

1. A short introduction, setting a mood of stillness.

2. A gently lilting melody played by the strings (A).

3. The main theme (B). This is a Norwegian folk tune, 'I Ola-Dalom, i Ola-Kjönn,' used also by Grieg in a piano piece. (You can see the beginning of Grieg's music at the bottom of the page.) This is repeated, then:

4. The soft, repeated call of the cuckoo is heard on the clarinet.

5. Delius continues to weave his music magically around the Norwegian folk tune (B). There are two more groups of cuckoo-calls.

6. Towards the end theme A is heard once more, followed by a brief, hushed *coda*, or ending.

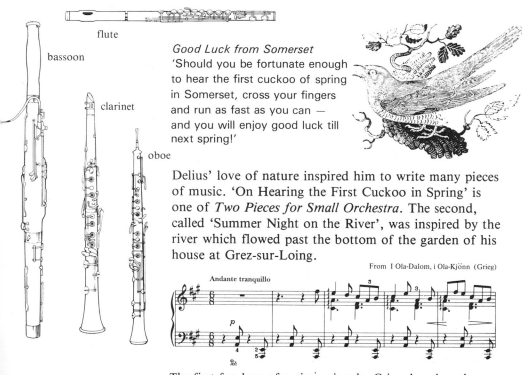

flute

bassoon

clarinet

oboe

Good Luck from Somerset
'Should you be fortunate enough to hear the first cuckoo of spring in Somerset, cross your fingers and run as fast as you can — and you will enjoy good luck till next spring!'

Delius' love of nature inspired him to write many pieces of music. 'On Hearing the First Cuckoo in Spring' is one of *Two Pieces for Small Orchestra*. The second, called 'Summer Night on the River', was inspired by the river which flowed past the bottom of the garden of his house at Grez-sur-Loing.

From I Ola-Dalom, i Ola-Kjönn (Grieg)

Andante tranquillo

The first few bars of a piano piece by Grieg, based on the same Norwegian folk-tune as Delius's 'First Cuckoo'.

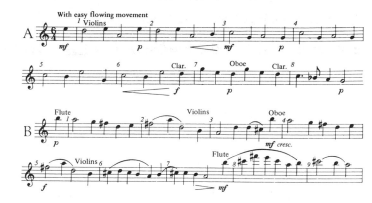

A — With easy flowing movement

B

Painting by Delius's wife of their garden, and the river at Grez-sur-Loing.

Ralph Vaughan Williams ENGLAND 1872-1958

Fantasia on Greensleeves

Ralph Vaughan Williams was born in the small Cotswold village of Down Ampney where his father was rector. His mother was a descendant of the famous Staffordshire pottery designer, Josiah Wedgwood.

As a composer, Vaughan Williams was a late starter. At the Royal College of Music in London, where he studied composition at the same time as Gustav Holst, he was not considered particularly promising. At the age of 36 he still felt that he had a lot to learn and went to Paris to take lessons from the French composer, Maurice Ravel, who orchestrated Mussorgsky's *Pictures at an Exhibition*. He made up for this late start, and continued to write music until his death, at the age of 86. In fact, five of his nine symphonies were written after the age of 70 — an interesting contrast to Sibelius who, though he lived to be 91, did not write much after he was 60.

Vaughan Williams became particularly interested in English folk tunes, and travelled about a great deal, collecting them and writing them down. One of his operas, *Sir John in Love*, is based on Shakespeare's play *The Merry Wives of Windsor*, which tells of the adventures of Sir John Falstaff. Vaughan Williams later took two of the old English tunes which he had used in this opera — 'Greensleeves' and 'Lovely Joan' — and wrote a short piece of music around them which he called *Fantasia on Greensleeves*. The music is written for 2 flutes, harp, and string orchestra (1st violins, 2nd violins, violas, cellos and double basses).

A village in the Cotswolds.

The viola and the double bass
The viola, like the violin, is tucked under the chin when it is played. It is slightly larger than the violin; the strings are tuned 5 notes lower, and the tone-colour is rather darker.

The double bass has sloping shoulders. It is so large that the player must either stand up, or perch upon a high stool. The strings are very long and thick, so that the notes are very low. When played with the bow, the tone is rather 'buzzier' than that of the cello; but when played *pizzicato* (plucked), the notes are full and round.

A

Greensleeves

A - las my love ___ you do me wrong ___ to cast me off ___ dis -

court - eous - ly, And I have lov - ed you so long ___ de -

light ing in ___ your com - pan - y. Green - sleeves ___ was

all my joy ___ Green - sleeves ___ was my de - light;

Green - sleeves was my heart of gold, ___ and who but my la - dy Green - sleeves.

B

Lovely Joan

Points to listen for

The music is in three sections with a short introduction.

1. Introduction. Flute and harp set a quiet pastoral mood.

2. After four soft harp chords, the 'Greensleeves' melody is heard played by 2nd violins and violas (A). Listen for the soft counter-melody higher up on 1st violins. Then the second half of the melody is repeated by the 1st violins.

3. Middle section. A sudden harp chord, and violins play *tremolo* — quick short up-and-down movements of the bow producing a 'trembling' effect. Violas and cellos play the other folk-tune 'Lovely Joan' (B).

4. Flutes repeat this tune with *pizzicato* accompaniment.

5. The tune is played for a third time above a jerky bass.

6. The 1st flute is heard playing alone, gently leading back to the same music as the beginning.

7. 'Greensleeves' is now played by the violas and cellos. When the 1st violins repeat the second half of the melody, they play an octave higher than previously.

The English folk-tune 'Greensleeves' is 400 years old at least and is twice mentioned in Shakespeare's play *The Merry Wives of Windsor*. The words and deeds of Sir John Falstaff are said to 'no more adhere and keep pace together than the Hundredth Psalm to the tune of *Greensleeves'*. Later in the play, Falstaff himself remarks: 'Let the sky rain potatoes; Let it thunder to the tune of *Greensleeves . . .*'

The flute

The flute is a tube about 26 inches long, usually made of metal but occasionally of wood. There is a hole in the side of the the instrument near one end. The player holds the flute horizontally and blows across this mouth-hole, so that the air inside the tube vibrates and makes the sound (rather like blowing across the top of a bottle). The lower notes sound soft and mellow, but the higher notes can be brilliantly clear.

The piccolo (Italian for 'tiny') is really a half-sized flute, with a high-pitched, brilliant sound.

The harp

A harp usually has 47 strings, some of gut and some of metal. These strings do not, in themselves, provide enough notes; and so the harp has seven pedals, one for each note of the scale. If the player presses a pedal down a notch, all the strings for those notes are shortened slightly, and so the notes sounded are one semi-tone higher. If the pedal is pressed down to the 2nd notch, the pitch is raised a further semi-tone. So the player is kept busy with his feet as well as with his hands. Two typical harp 'effects' are *arpeggios* — spreading out the notes of a chord one after the other; and the *glissando* — a quick sweeping of the fingers in a circular motion across the strings.

Mikhail Ippolitov-Ivanov RUSSIA 1859-1935

The Procession of the Sardar

Ippolitov-Ivanov attended the Music Academy at St. Petersburg where he studied orchestration under the Russian composer Rimsky-Korsakov. He spent many years in the Caucasus, a mountainous region east of the Black Sea. There he discovered and wrote down the strange folk melodies of the people.

He is best known for his *Four Caucasian Sketches* of which 'The Procession of the Sardar' is the final piece. It is a musical picture of a camel-train, guarded by fierce warriors, winding its way through the Caucasus with the Sardar — a chieftain — at its head.

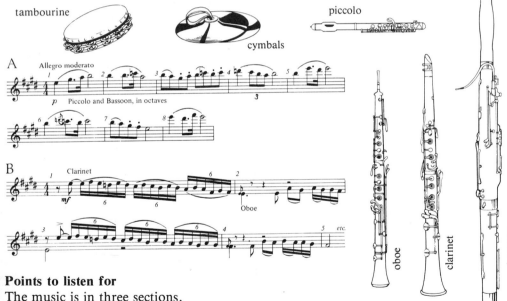

Points to listen for
The music is in three sections.

1. Percussion and French horns begin an intriguing rhythm. Piccolo and bassoon give the tune an eastern flavour (A).

2. A clarinet decorates the oboe melody of the middle section (B) while the tambourine keeps the rhythm going. There is a stirring climax of brass fanfares with crashing cymbals. A slight pause, then:

3. Tune A triumphantly returns, now made even more exciting by a slightly faster pace.

Quiz 1

(Only 'cheat' — by looking back for an answer — if you really have to!)

1. Musical similes
Can you complete these?
a) As bold as . . .
b) As fit as a . . .
c) As clear as a . . .
d) As clean as a . . .
e) As tight as a . . .

Complete these, then mention a piece of music (together with its composer) in connection with each one.
a) As strong as an . . .
b) As brave as a . . .
c) As hungry as a . . .
d) As busy as a . . .

2. Which instrument?
Here are some anagrams — or jumbled words. Each one is an instrument.
a) CLEAR TIN   g) BUS — ALSO BED
b) PERT TUM   h) AIR TUG
c) O PAIN!   i) COAL GRAINS
d) GROAN!   j) MINI TAP
e) MOOR BENT   k) REAL TING!
f) A SOB SON   l) OUT, ME BAIRN!

3. Instrumental roll-call
Can you name . . .
a) 1 instrument beginning with *x*?
b) 1 instrument beginning with *w*?
c) 2 instruments beginning with *o*?
d) 2 more beginning with *f*?
e) 3 instruments beginning with *h*?
f) 4 (or more — there are at least 8!) beginning with *t*?

4. Who wrote what?
Decode the following to discover 6 composers and 6 countries. Then arrange them in matching pairs, each composer next to his own country. (The code is: A = 1; B = 2; C = 3; and so on.)
a) 13-21-19-19-15-18-7-19-11-25
b) 3-26-5-3-8-15-19-12-15-22-1-11-9-1
c) 6-18-1-14-3-5
d) 19-9-2-5-12-9-21-19
e) 4-5-12-9-21-19
f) 18-21-19-19-9-1
g) 7-18-9-5-7
h) 6-9-14-12-1-14-4
i) 5-14-7-12-1-14-4
j) 19-1-9-14-20-19-1-5-14-19
k) 19-13-5-20-1-14-1
l) 14-15-18-23-1-25

5. Which section?
To which section of the orchestra do these instruments belong?
a) Violin   d) Cello   g) Xylophone
b) Flute   e) Cor anglais h) Saxophone
c) Harp   f) Tuba

6. In plain English
Can you give the English meaning for each of these foreign words?
a) *Pizzicato* d) *Cor anglais* g) *Suomi*
b) *Coda*   e) *Forte*   h) *Bydlo*
c) *Timpani*   f) *Piano*

7. Any other name . . .
Can you match the names?

Bedřich	Sibelius
Jean	Delius
Modeste	Grieg
Edvard	Smetana
Frederick	Mussorgsky

8. Musical chains
The last letter of each answer is the first letter of the next.
A a) Italian for 'plucked'.
  b) Seasonal piece by English composer.
  c) Norwegian composer.
  d) Well-known English folk-melody.
  e) Finnish composer.
B a) Another name for kettle-drum.
  b) Composer of *Procession of the Sardar*.
  c) English composer.
  d) This composer wrote *Danse Macabre*.
  e) The kind of bird which glided upon the waters of Tuonela.
  f) Grieg's nationality.
C a) This instrument imitates clattering bones in *Danse Macabre*.
  b) Country of Vaughan Williams's birth.
  c) He composed *On Hearing the First Cuckoo in Spring*.
  d) This instrument represents the minstrel in Mussorgsky's 'The Old Castle'.
  e) The instrument which sings the sad song of Sibelius's Swan—in English!

9. More anagrams
Rearrange the letters of these words to find the answers. There are clues to help you.
a) LEG VERSE SEEN — well-known melody used by Vaughan-Williams (1 word).
b) LET COAST HELD — one of Mussorgsky's 'Pictures' (3 words).
c) HAND TRUE LOG—name of a composer's house on a fjord (1 word).
d) A HUT WAS OFTEN LONE—by a composer from a similar country (4 words).
e) LET'S HUG HONEST WOLF — another of Mussorgsky's pictures (5 words).
f) BARE CANS MADE — even at midnight? (? words).

Claude Debussy FRANCE 1862-1918
Fêtes
from Nocturnes

Claude Debussy was born in Paris of very poor parents. His mother taught him to read and write, but even when he had reached middle age, Debussy's spelling was atrocious.

As a boy, he was fascinated by the sea. (One of his most important compositions was three orchestral pieces entitled *La Mer* — The Sea.) His father wanted him to join the French Navy, but an aunt arranged piano lessons for him and he showed such promise that, at the age of ten, he began to study at the Paris Conservatoire. Here, however, his unconventional ideas about music made him rather unpopular with his teachers.

When he was 18, he was engaged by Madame Nadezhda von Meck — a wealthy Russian noblewoman who was Tchaikovsky's friend and patroness — to travel through Italy and Switzerland with her, acting as music teacher to her family. She sent one of Debussy's compositions to Tchaikovsky who was rather severe in his criticism of what, to him, seemed rather strange music. Debussy fell in love with Madame von Meck's 16-year-old daughter Sonia, who was one of Russia's richest heiresses, and suggested marriage. But the offer was refused. He married a Parisian seamstress called Lili Texier. At first, his music brought him very little money; even on his wedding day he was so poor that he had to give piano lessons in order to pay for the wedding breakfast!

In the late 19th century French composers were trying to strike out in a new direction. At that time a group of painters called the Impressionists were experimenting with new ways of painting. Instead of trying to make their paintings look 'real' as in a photograph, these painters merely gave an *impression* of what the eye might take in at a single glance — an impression of hazy outlines, and especially the play of shimmering light and movement. Poets, too, such as Paul Verlaine, attempted to produce this kind of effect with words. You can read the first verse of his poem *Chanson d'Automne* ('Song of Autumn') on the page opposite. The poem suggests the melancholy mood of Autumn without actually describing it.

Debussy became very interested in the idea of Impressionism and used the same technique in music — broad washes of shimmering sounds with bright splashes of instrumental colour.

To the Impressionists — whether painters, poets, or musicians — *atmosphere* is very important, and light and shade are carefully balanced.

The Houses of Parliament, by the impressionist painter Monet.

> I explained to Debussy the necessity for a Frenchman to free himself from the influence of Wagner... Why could we not use the same means as Monet, Cézanne and Toulouse-Lautrec?
>
> (The French composer, Eric Satie)

Between 1894 and 1899, Debussy wrote three orchestral pieces in Impressionist style. At first, he intended to score them for violin and orchestra and call them 'Studies in Grey', but he changed his mind, writing for orchestra only and calling the pieces *Nocturnes*. This is how he described the music:

'The title "Nocturne" does not refer to the usual *nocturne* (a night-piece with a hushed atmosphere) but rather to all the various impressions and effects of light the work implies . . .'

And this is how he explains the second piece which is called *Fêtes,* or 'Festivals':

'Movement, rhythm which dances in the atmosphere with sudden flashes of light. There is also a section with a procession which winds in and out of the Festival and mingles with it. But the main idea is the Festival itself and the music which is woven into it like a luminous haze . . .'

Claude Debussy.

Clarinets and Cor Anglais (A)

Oboe (B)

Flutes, Oboes and Clarinets (C)

Muted Trumpet (D)

flute

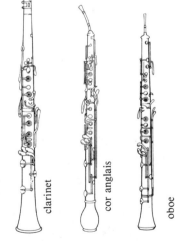

clarinet

cor anglais

oboe

muted trumpet

Chanson d'Automne
Les sanglots longs
Des violons
De l'automne
Blessent mon coeur
D'une langueur
Monotone.

(Song of Autumn)

The long drawn sobs
Of the violins
Of Autumn
Wound my heart
With a monotonous
Languor.

(Paul Verlaine)

Points to listen for

1. Violins set the rhythm for a gay winding dance on the woodwind (A).

2. A brass fanfare; then a swirl of harp (a *glissando*) leads to a variation of the theme with 15 beats to a bar, causing the music to press forward. Woven into the dancing rhythms of the orchestra, among the shimmering and shifting colours, light and movement, listen especially for:

3. A rhythmic theme on the oboe (B);

4. And a more flowing melody for woodwind (C) with rhythms drawn across the bar-lines, later taken over joyfully by the strings.

5. Then harps, kettle-drums, and pizzicato strings tread a soft, mysterious march-rhythm with a theme on muted trumpets (D), quietly at first, as if a procession is approaching in the far distance.

6. The procession draws nearer as theme D is now played by the woodwind; then loudly by the brass with exciting snare drum rhythms and cymbals, while violins play a version of theme A high above.

7. A return to the rather quieter music of the opening mood.

8. Listen for reminders of the muted trumpet theme (D).

9. A slow, quiet passage played rather wistfully by the oboe.

10. A final reminder of the festivities, *pianissimo*, as if now in the distance.

The Little Train of the Caipira

from Bachianas Brasileiras No. 2

Brazil is the largest country in South America. The river Amazon — one of the world's largest rivers — rises in the Andes Mountains of Peru, then flows almost 4,000 miles eastwards across Brazil to the Atlantic Ocean.

The capital was once Rio de Janeiro, on the Atlantic coast, but since 1960 has been Brasilia, 600 miles north-west in the heart of Brazil. Until 1960, the interior was almost uninhabited. Even now, though certain parts of Brazil are very highly developed, there is still a vast area of tropical rain forest inhabited only by a few tribes.

Villa-Lobos is Brazil's most important composer. He has written a great deal of music of all kinds — about 2000 pieces. As a boy he spent so much time at the piano that his mother sold it. But he managed to get hold of a guitar and continued his musical studies in secret. Later, to make money, he played in cafes and theatre orchestras, and at one time worked in a factory, making matches. Like many composers — such as Smetana, Grieg and Vaughan Williams — he firmly believed the music of a country should have its own national flavour. And so he set out to explore the interior of Brazil, following the course of the river Amazon, in search of folk music. He not only collected melodies and rhythms from the Indian tribes, but also brought back many folk instruments. Many of his pieces use these authentic Brazilian instruments whose sounds cannot be imitated by the more usual orchestral instruments.

Villa-Lobos wrote several pieces in which he tried to combine Brazilian folk melodies and rhythms with the flavour of the music of Bach. He called these *Bachianas Brasileiras,* or 'Brazilian Bach-Music'. The second of these ends with a piece describing the journey of 'The Little Train of the Caipira'.

View over the bay of Rio de Janeiro.

Here is the approximate timing, in minutes and seconds, of the journey of the Little Train of the Caipira (Brazilian word for peasant) as it winds its way through the interior of Brazil:

00.00   Departure of the Little Train. A variety of interesting percussion instruments, especially *maracas* (hollow gourds with dried seeds inside which rattle) and *guiro* (a large gourd, sounded by scraping a stick over notches cut into the surface). The Little Train gathers speed . . .

00.35   Violins sing a melody above the rhythm of the train as it chatters and clatters along (see music).

01.21   Clarinets suggest the wailing whistle, as the Little Train importantly warns of its approach.

01.41   The music changes gear — as if the Little Train is bravely about to tackle a particularly hilly section.

01.56   The melody is now sung by woodwind instruments, with busy clankings from the percussion.

02.52   Warning hoots on brass instruments. Trills from the woodwind.

03.02   Finally, at great length, and with a good deal of fuss, the Little Train begins to slow to a halt with a hiss of escaping steam (maracas) and the squeal of brakes on metal wheels (whistling harmonics on high violins).

03.58   Arrival of the Little Train of the Caipira.

A Brazilian native dance.

Maracas.

Sometimes, Villa-Lobos used fragments of the native languages of the tribes he discovered. On other occasions he made up his own words based on these sounds to create a folk atmosphere. Some pieces imitate the sounds of the Brazilian interior. The second part of *Bachianas Brasileiras No. 5,* for soprano and 8 cellos, suggests the sounds of birds in the Brazilian jungle.

Richard Wagner GERMANY 1813—1883

𝕿he 𝕽ide of the 𝖁alkyries

In 1853, Wagner began to compose a cycle of four operas called *The Ring* in which he used material from both Scandinavian and German mythology. The second opera in the cycle is called 'The Valkyries'.

In Norse mythology, the Valkyries were fierce warrior daughters of Wotan, the chief god. They rode down through the clouds on horse-back and snatched up the bodies of heroes who had fallen in battle, and took them up to Valhalla, the home of the gods, to an accompaniment of thunder and lightning.

The complete cycle of *The Ring* was first performed on four successive evenings as Wagner intended. The occasion was the opening of the new opera house at Bayreuth, built to Wagner's own design. By that time, Wagner had won fame all over Europe and was living fairly comfortably. But before that, he had been constantly in debt and had had to disappear several times to escape angry creditors. On another occasion, Wagner was in serious trouble for having a hand in a political uprising in Dresden.

Cartoon of Wagner conducting.

A warrant for Wagner's arrest issued in Dresden in May 1849.

♪ Points to listen for

The scene is a rugged mountain peak. A storm is breaking as the Valkyries, clad in glittering armour and carrying spears and shields, prepare to mount their horses. The music vividly describes their wild ride through the storm. Against a background of rising and falling scales in the strings, with trills from the woodwind, the mighty theme can be heard in the brass.

1. Horns play the 'riding' motive (A), to be heard throughout the music.

2. The mighty theme of the Valkyries (B), played mainly by trombones.

3. Eventually the war-cry of the Valkyries is heard (C).

4. Theme B is heard again.

5. Descending scales on strings and woodwind, as with unearthly shrieks the Valkyries plunge through the clouds. Kettle-drums imitate the rhythm of hoof-beats, while cymbals suggest flashes of lightning.

6. Theme B returns, with the 'riding' motive played by 8 French horns.

7. Theme B once more, with a double-bass tuba to add even more power.

8. A reminder of the war-cry (C). Then a swift, rushing conclusion.

The trombone

This instrument is more than 600 years old. The early name for it was *sackbut*. It is the only instrument in the brass section without valves. Instead it has a *slide* which the player slides in and out to alter the length of the tube. There are seven positions for the slide, each with its own range of notes which the player obtains by means of lip pressure. For special effects, the trombone can be muted, or the player can play a *glissando* by sliding the tube in or out and blowing at the same time. There are usually 3 trombones in an orchestra — 2 tenors, and 1 bass.

The kettle-drum

The kettle-drum (the Italian word is *timpani*) is the most important instrument in the percussion section. It is a copper bowl, with a skin stretched across the top. Around the rim are 6 T-shaped screws which can tighten or slacken the skin, and so alter the note. A player is often asked to change the pitch during a piece of music, so he must turn the screws and listen softly for the note he requires while the rest of the orchestra is playing. Some modern kettle-drums have a foot pedal to change the pitch more easily. The player can play single notes; or he can play a *roll* by using both sticks alternately and very quickly. There are usually 3 or 4 kettle-drums in an orchestra.

Here is how 'The Ride of the Valkyries' was staged in Paris in the 1890's. Large wooden models of the Valkyries on horseback were drawn along a huge wooden scaffolding by means of a cable. Storm clouds, painted on revolving glass discs, were projected onto a gauze hung in front, adding depth and realism. The effect of the light upon the gauze was to mask the scaffolding but still to allow the Valkyries to be seen.

The picture below shows how the audience would have seen it.

A contemporary cartoon suggesting how Wagner obtained his sound effects.

Wagner found the normal-sized orchestra inadequate for his needs when he was composing *The Ring*. 'The Ride of the Valkyries' is scored for: 2 piccolos, 2 flutes, 3 oboes, cor anglais, 3 clarinets, bass clarinet, 3 bassoons, 8 horns, 3 trumpets, 4 trombones, double-bass tuba, 2 pairs of kettle-drums, triangle, cymbals, tenor drum, and strings.

At first, the strange sounds from Wagner's immense orchestra caused some disturbance among listeners, as the cartoons on this page show.

Gioacchino Rossini ITALY 1792-1868

Overture to William Tell

Most countries have a national hero — or more than one. You might think of Robin Hood, for instance, as an English national hero.

The Swiss national hero is William Tell, who lived towards the end of the 14th century, at a time when Switzerland was ruled by Austria. A man called Gessler harshly governed the Swiss in the name of the Austrian Emperor. He hung his hat on a pole and ordered that all should bow to it in recognition of his authority. William Tell refused. Gessler arrested Tell with his son Jemmy and forced him to shoot an arrow through an apple placed upon the boy's head. Tell split the apple cleanly into two pieces. Gessler noticed another arrow half-hidden beneath Tell's cloak. When he asked what the second arrow was for, Tell replied that it would have split Gessler's heart if Jemmy had been harmed. Instead of allowing Tell to go free, Gessler ordered him to be taken to a dungeon on the far side of Lake Lucerne, but a violent storm blew up and Tell escaped.

Tell did shoot an arrow through Gessler's heart and then encouraged the Swiss to revolt and drive the Austrians out of their country.

Early in the 19th century, the German poet and dramatist, Schiller, wrote a play about the story. In 1892, the Italian composer, Rossini, wrote an opera based on Schiller's play.

16th century woodcut of William Tell shooting the apple.

When Rossini composed *William Tell* he had already written nearly 40 operas, and was the most famous operatic composer of the day. This was to be his last opera. After completing it, at the age of 37, he 'retired' — and though he lived for another 39 years, he wrote no more works for the stage. Just why this was, nobody really knows. Some people think that he was afraid of failure; others, that he was worn out by the busy life he had led. 'I have a passion for idleness,' he told a friend, 'just as you have a passion for work!'

Points to listen for

An operatic overture is a piece played by the orchestra before the curtain rises, often using tunes from the opera which follows. But Rossini's overture to his opera *William Tell* is more than just an introduction to the opera; it is more like a tone poem (music which tells a story, or paints a picture in sound). The music is in four sections; unfortunately, the famous episode where William Tell shoots the apple is not included.

1. Introduction. The rich tone colours of 5 solo cellos, accompanied by the rest of the cellos, double basses and kettle-drums, paint a serene sunrise over the Alps near Lake Lucerne (A; later, B).

2. Alpine storm. Rustling strings suggest the rising wind as the first spatters of rain are heard on the woodwind. Then the storm breaks in sudden fury. Listen specially for wild trombones, and bass drum, effectively used to imitate thunder echoing among the mountain crags. With a rumble of strings and kettle-drums, the storm fades away in the distance . . .

3. Shepherds on the mountain-side. First, the clear tone of the flute paints blue skies after the storm. Then the cor anglais imitates a cow-herd playing the 'Ranz des Vaches', a Swiss pastoral melody, on an alpine horn. Later, the flute decorations suggest the song of a bird, hovering and fluttering, while the triangle imitates the peaceful yet desolate sound of cow-bells (C).

4. Revolution. The peace is shattered by a sudden fanfare of trumpets and horns (D) which introduces an exciting rhythmic gallop (E), describing the Swiss overthrow of the Austrian invaders. This is in the style of a typical Rossini 'crescendo', beginning quietly but increasing in power and excitement as more and more instruments join in.

William Tell monument at Altdorf, Switzerland.

The Hungarian pianist and composer, Franz Liszt, once played the overture to *William Tell* on the piano to an audience of lunatics in an asylum, but had to be stopped during the final gallop due to their over-excitement!

Peter Tchaikovsky RUSSIA 1840-1893

1812 Overture

for full orchestra, military band, bells and cannon

In 1812, Napoleon's army advanced upon Moscow. Rather than suffer defeat by the French, the Russians burned their own city and withdrew. When the French army arrived there was neither food nor shelter. Napoleon was forced to retreat — defeated by the bitter weather rather than by the Russians.

Frozen, starving and exhausted, the French army limped across the snow-covered wastes. Many hundreds of soldiers died on the way. Here is how a survivor described the Retreat from Moscow:

'Whenever we stopped to eat hastily, the horses left behind were bled. The blood was caught in a saucepan, cooked and eaten. But often we were forced to eat it before there was time to cook it . . . The saucepan was carried with us, and each man, as he marched, dipped his hands in and took what he wanted; his face in consequence became smeared with blood . . . Those on foot dragged themselves painfully along, almost all of them having their feet frozen and wrapped in rags or in bits of sheepskin, and all nearly dying of hunger . . .'

68 years later, in 1880, the Cathedral of Christ the Redeemer in Moscow was nearing completion. It was to be consecrated in thanksgiving for the French defeat of 1812, and Tchaikovsky was asked to compose a piece of music for the occasion.

Realising that a rather spectacular work was called for, he composed a lengthy overture for full orchestra, military band, bells and cannon. (An operatic overture, such as *William Tell,* is intended to be played at the beginning of an opera; a concert-overture is a separate piece, usually opening an orchestral concert.)

Napoleon watching the burning of Moscow from the Kremlin.

'The Retreat from Moscow' by Meissonier.

The music has many contrasting themes: themes which Tchaikovsky may have based upon Cossack songs and folk tunes from the Novgorod region; exciting fanfares; an old Czarist hymn-tune; the French national anthem, the 'Marseillaise'; and the national anthem of Czarist Russia.

In a letter to his friend, Madame Nadezhda von Meck, Tchaikovsky described the overture as 'very noisy, with no great artistic value', having been composed 'without much enthusiasm'. But in spite of the composer's own comments, the *1812 Overture* enjoys great popularity all over the world.

The *1812 Overture* was originally to have been performed by a massive orchestra outside the Cathedral, with a whole battery of guns to be fired at the appropriate moment by means of wires attached to the conductor's stand! Towards the end, all the bells of Moscow were to ring out. Unfortunately, the performance never took place. Instead the work was played — without the special effects — at an exhibition in Moscow two years later, in 1882.

Points to listen for

1. The overture begins quietly with an old Czarist hymn-tune played by 2 solo violas and 4 solo cellos (A).

2. Woodwind instruments join in, then strings accompany a plaintive oboe melody (B).

3. The pace quickens as the brass enters.

4. A section marked *andante* (at a walking pace). To a rhythm on the snare drum, oboes, clarinets and horns play a fanfare-like theme (C).

5. The tempo (or pace) changes to *allegro* (lively—and fairly fast). A strongly rhythmic theme for strings (D).

6. The excitement grows until the horns hint at the melody of the Marseillaise (E)(i), heard more completely afterwards on 2 cornets (E)(ii). Some scurrying passages for woodwind and strings are heard. (Notice that the melodic outline of the horn phrase is similar to the opening of the fanfare-like theme C).

7. A more tranquil melody for violins and violas (F) with triangle, and chords on woodwind and brass.

8. A Russian folk tune follows, scored for flute and clarinet with a rhythmic tambourine accompaniment (G).

9. The music becomes more stormy with a reappearance of the strongly rhythmic theme (D) and the horn phrase (E)(i). Listen for the fragments of the 'Marseillaise'.

10. The excitement dies down and the tranquil theme is heard again (F).

11. A brief return of the rhythmic folksong (G).

12. The pace is whipped up again with the 'Marseillaise' theme (E)(ii). Another climax—and the first cannon effects. The 'Marseillaise' appears to triumph, but is suddenly drowned by massive descending scales on woodwind and strings, leading to:

13. The Czarist hymn-tune played *fff* by woodwind, brass and military band, to the triumphant accompaniment of pealing bells.

14. Then the music is brought to a blazing conclusion with the fanfare-like theme (C), now marked *ffff*, and the final triumph of the national anthem of Czarist Russia (H), punctuated by cannon-fire.

Felix Mendelssohn GERMANY 1809-1847

Overture -The Hebrides (Fingal's cave)

Fingal's cave can only be approached from the sea. At high tide the waves crash into its mouth, while seabirds wheel and skim, uttering sharp piercing cries. During his stay in Scotland in 1829, at the age of 20, Mendelssohn visited Fingal's cave with his friend, Klingermann. It proved to be a rough journey — and Mendelssohn was a poor sailor. But he was sufficiently impressed by the wild beauty to jot down a few bars of music, which were later to become the opening of the *Hebrides Overture*. Klingermann later remarked that Mendelssohn's musical mind was on far better terms with the sea than his stomach was! Mendelssohn included the scrap of music in a letter which he sent home to his family, saying: 'In order to make you understand how extraordinary the Hebrides have affected me, the following came into my mind there.'

Arriving back at the house where he was staying, Mendelssohn immediately made for the piano to try out the ideas which had occurred to him — only to be told that it was Sunday and music, therefore, was out of the question. However, by means of his charm and persuasion, he was able to overcome this difficulty and set to work. The *Hebrides Overture,* also known as 'Fingal's Cave', began to take shape . . .

Points to listen for

1. The music begins peacefully with a theme on violas, cellos and bassoons (A). The murmur of the sea, gently rising and falling. This is soon taken over by the violins.

2. A 'bridge passage', built upon a short phrase (B), leads to the second theme.

3. This is more flowing and lyrical (C). It is first played by cellos, clarinets and bassoons beneath wavy decorations on the upper strings, then repeated by the violins.

4. The first theme (A) returns in the woodwind, and is used to build up a climax. This section ends with fanfares on the woodwind and brass.

5. Then follows the 'development' section. It is here that previously heard ideas are worked out in more detail. The texture of the music becomes rougher, as if a storm threatens, whipping the sea to a fury and forcing waves to crash into the cave. Fanfare-like figures on the brass, suggesting the desolate cries of seabirds, are echoed by the woodwind — just as sounds would echo inside the cave itself. There are sharp contrasts of *forte* and *piano; staccato* (crisp and detached) and *legato* (smooth); long-held notes against quicker-moving parts. Listen for all three ideas, A, B and C, and a very rhythmic passage in which wind and strings answer each other (based on theme A).

6. The development ends with a thunderous crash on the kettle-drum and a run-up on the flutes, as if a mighty wave crashes into the cave, sending spray hurtling into the air.

7. The more tranquil mood of the opening returns. Themes A and C are heard once more, but theme C is this time given to the clarinet.

8. A *coda* rounds off the piece. The sea again becomes angry, with a great deal of quick playing on the strings. But the final three bars are peaceful.

Painters and writers, too, have been similarly affected by the Hebrides. In the poem above you can read how the novelist, Sir Walter Scott, recorded his impression of the Isle of Staffa. And here is how the poet, John Keats, described the beauty and mystery of Fingal's Cave:

'The shores of Mull on the eastward lay
And Ulva dark and Colonsay,
And all the group of islets gay
That guard famed Staffa round.
Then all unknown its columns rose,
Where dark and undisturbed repose
The cormorant had found,
And the shy seal had quiet home,
And weltered in that wondrous dome,
Where Nature herself, it seemed, would raise
A Minster to her Maker's praise!
Not for a meaner use ascend
Her columns, or her arches bend;
Nor of a theme less solemn tells
That mighty surge that ebbs and swells.'
(Sir Walter Scott).

> 'Suppose, now, the giants who came down to the daughters of men had taken a whole mass of these columns and bound them together like bunches of matches, and then with immense axes had made a cavern in the body of these columns. Such is Fingal's Cave, except that the sea has done the work of excavation and is continually dashing there. The colour of the columns is a sort of black with a lurking gloom of purple therein. For solemnity and grandeur it far surpasses the finest cathedral.'
>
> (John Keats)

Benjamin Britten ENGLAND 1913-1976

Four Sea Interludes *from* Peter Grimes

Britten's opera *Peter Grimes* is a tragic drama about the sea and fisherfolk. It is based upon actual events described in a poem called *The Borough* by the 18th century poet, George Crabbe. Crabbe was born on the coast of East Anglia, not far from Britten's home, at Aldeburgh. He became a country clergyman and recorded his observations of village life in a collection of poems.

As the opera begins, the townsfolk suspect that Grimes has murdered his apprentice. They try unsuccessfully to prevent him from getting a new one. When he ill-treats the second apprentice, called John, the people decide to take action. As Grimes hears them approaching his hut, he hustles the boy out of the cliff-side door. But as John is scrambling down the cliff he misses his footing and falls to his death. Grimes loses his reason as the mob pursues him, convinced that he has murdered this apprentice as well. He puts out to sea and drowns himself . . .

The beach at Aldeburgh.

Peter Grimes and his new apprentice (scene from the opera).

'For most of my life I have lived closely in touch with the sea. My parents' house in Lowestoft directly faced the sea, and my life as a child was coloured by the fierce storms that sometimes drove ships onto our coast and ate away whole stretches of the neighbouring cliffs. In writing *Peter Grimes* I wanted to express my awareness of the perpetual struggle of men and women whose livelihood depends on the sea . . .'

(Benjamin Britten)

The townsfolk plan to take action (scene from the opera).

An interlude in an opera is a piece of music played by the orchestra while the curtain is down. For *Peter Grimes* Britten composed six interludes: three to introduce the three acts, and three more to be played between the first and second scene of each act. He has chosen four of these interludes to be played together as a concert piece. Each one does more than just entertain the audience while the scenery is changed; each piece adds something dramatic to the atmosphere of the story.

1. Dawn

In the opera, this interlude is played between the Prologue and Act I. A cold, grey morning. The fisherfolk are busy baiting lines, repairing nets and sails.

The music is entirely based on the three ideas heard at the beginning (**A**). Desolate violins and flutes, very high, play a phrase followed by a bubbling *arpeggio* on clarinets, violas and harp. This is answered by dark, sustained chords on the brass, bassoons and lower strings with a rumble of bass drum and kettle-drums.

A suggestion of a fresh breeze and the lapping of cold, grey water. The sea, almost at rest — but the brass reminds us of the constant threat of its power and cruelty.

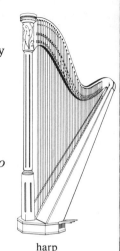
harp

viola

2. Sunday Morning

This music introduces Act II. Sunlight glistens on the ever-moving water, and there is an impression of church bells as the townsfolk pass along the street on their way to church.

1. Sustained chords played by 4 French horns are soon joined by a joyfully rhythmic theme (**B**) — first on high woodwind instruments; then on high strings.

2. The second theme (**C**) offers a complete contrast: smooth-toned violas and cellos above a rhythmic bass, while flute and piccolo weave chirping decorations high above.

3. Tune B returns, now with trumpets added so that it sounds even more joyful than before. A deep church bell begins to toll — suggested by a B flat tubular bell, gong, harp, bassoons, trombones, tuba, and double basses.

4. The bell continues to toll as Tune C is heard again.

5. As the large bell ceases, a smaller bell begins to toll — an E flat tubular bell reinforced by French horns — rather quicker, as if urging the people to come to church. Against this can be heard the disjointed rhythms of Tune B, followed by Tune C which soars high on the violins above soft, misty discords.

3. Moonlight

A peaceful introduction to Act III. The street at night. The dark beauty of the scene is evoked by a sustained theme on the cellos (D). When this is repeated, flickers of flutes and harp suggest moonlight silvering the roof-tops and the crests of gently moving waves. There is a slight hint of menace as the music becomes more disturbed. Then a return to the opening mood of beauty and stillness.

4. Storm

An interlude played between scenes 1 and 2 of Act I. The music is menacing, suggesting the power and cruelty of the sea.

1. Wild rhythms dominated by theme E on the lower woodwind and strings, with pounding kettle-drums.

2. Theme F — first on snarling trombones, then on trumpets.

3. Theme E again on the strings.

4. High, screaming woodwind suggest the wind whipping above the fury of the storm (G).

5. An angry, triumphant outburst on brass and percussion.

6. A lull in the storm. An upwards sweep on the harp introduces a theme for the violins (H).

7. Rising strings against woodwind and tambourine.

8. Theme H is heard again.

9. A reminder of the first theme (E). Then a pounding, terrifying conclusion.

'Hark to those sounds! They're from distress at sea!
How quick they come! What terrors may there be . . .
From parted clouds the moon her radiance throws
On the wild waves, and all the danger shows;
But shows them beaming in her shining vest,
Terrific splendour! Gloom in glory dress'd!
This for a moment, and then clouds again
Hide every beam, and fear and darkness reign . . .'

(from *The Borough* by George Crabbe)

Quiz 2

(Only 'cheat' — by looking back for an answer — if you really have to!)

1. Which instrument?
a) A brass instrument which has no valves.
b) A plucked string instrument similar to the guitar and the banjo.
c) Another plucked string instrument, similar to a guitar but pear-shaped, and popular in Tudor times.
d) This woodwind instrument (in English!) plays the melancholy song of Sibelius's *Swan of Tuonela*.
e) The 'curly' member of the brass section.
(When you have answered these questions, take the first letter only of each answer. When rearranged, the letters will spell yet another instrument.)

2. In plain English
Can you give the English meaning for each of these foreign words?
a) Fortissimo
b) Pianissimo
c) Staccato
d) Legato
e) Nocturne
f) Coda
g) Andante
h) Allegro

3. Who am I?
Identify each of these composers and the pieces of music they describe:
a) I wrote a noisy piece of music including cannon and bells.
b) I wrote a quiet piece of music about the countryside in spring.
c) I wrote an overture about my visit to Scotland.
d) I wrote an opera about a Swiss hero.

4. Musical anagrams
A These are composers:
a) NETTRIB
b) WRENGA
c) BYSEDSU
d) SINORIS
e) BLOLILASOV
f) VOKISTYKACH
(Can you give the Christian name of each one?)

B These are countries:
a) YATLI
b) LAZRIB
c) GRAYMEN
d) FERCAN
e) SARIUS
f) DENLANG
(Now match each country to the correct composer, and mention a piece of music by each one.)

C These are instruments:
a) I'M IN TAP
b) ROB ME NOT!
c) SING PEEL LOCK
d) NOX HY POLE
(To which section of the orchestra does each one belong?)

D And these are titles:
a) TILL I AM WELL
b) VALSE IN ACFG
c) HORSE! DRIVE! FLY A KITE!
(Give the composer of each one, with his nationality.)

5. What am I?
a) I am a woodwind instrument with a French name.
b) I am a drum which can be tuned to give a certain note.
c) I am a brass instrument with a slide instead of valves.
d) I have strips of wood which are hit with sticks.
e) I am a woodwind instrument with a single reed, but am made of brass not wood.
f) I am the smallest member of the woodwind section.

6. Musical chains
The last letter of each answer is the first letter of the next.
A a) Name of Wagner's 'cycle' of four operas.
b) William Tell's enemy.
c) Composer of the opera *William Tell*.
d) The same composer's nationality.
e) He ordered the Retreat from Moscow.
B a) Villa-Lobos's country.
b) The Italian word for 'smoothly'.
c) *1812* and *Fingal's Cave* are kinds of . . .
d) The country where Britten was born.
e) The first of Britten's *Sea Interludes*.
C a) Another name for *timpani*.
b) Composer of the *Hebrides Overture*.
c) Debussy's piece called *Fêtes* is one of a set of three. The set is called . . .
d) Rough music by Britten.
e) The type of band used in *1812*.

7. Who wrote what?
Match the correct composer to each title.

Four Sea Interludes	Mendelssohn
1812 Overture	Saint-Saëns
Fêtes	Rossini
Fingal's Cave	Sibelius
William Tell Overture	Smetana
Danse Macabre	Debussy
Vltava	Wagner
Finlandia	Britten
The Ride of the Valkyries	Tchaikovsky

8. Solve the codes
Can you decode these sentences?
a) LTSDR LZX AD TRDC NM DHSGDQ AQZRR NQ RSQHMF HMRSQTLDMSR.
b) BOPUIFS OBNF GPS 'UIF IFCSJEFT PWFSUVSF' JT 'GJOHBM'T DBWF'.
c) RKBBKECVQ KU CP KVCNKCP YQTF OGCPKPI 'RNWEMGF'.

Johann Sebastian Bach GERMANY 1685-1750

Brandenburg Concerto No. 2 in F major

Bach belonged to one of the most amazing families in the history of music. We can trace the family for over 200 years, and of the 60 Bachs known to us by name, 53 were talented musicians. Bach himself married twice, and his two wives between them had no less than 20 children — several of them very able composers and performers.

Bach's parents both died before he was ten years old, so he went to live with his eldest brother. He used to creep downstairs when the household was asleep and copy out music by moonlight. One night his brother discovered him. The music was locked away, but the boy kept his interest in music and learned to play the organ.

When he was 18, Bach became organist at the town of Arnstadt in Germany. He was not very popular. People accused him of making his organ accompaniments too elaborate, and also he had 'allowed a strange young girl to visit the organ loft, and even play music in the church'. The 'strange young girl' was, in fact, his cousin, Maria Barbara, whom he married a year or so later.

To earn their living, composers often used to take posts at the courts of rich noblemen and wrote music specially for their orchestras. In 1717 Bach became conductor of the orchestra at the court of Prince Leopold of Anhalt-Cöthen. It was there that he met a court singer, Anna Magdalena, who became his second wife in 1721. That same year he wrote six orchestral concertos, dedicated to another rich nobleman 'His Princely Highness, the Margrave of Brandenburg'. The Margrave must have failed to appreciate the Concertos for they were later discovered tied up in a dusty parcel, instead of being neatly filed in the court library. They are the ones now known as the *Brandenburg Concertos*.

Towards the end of his busy life, Bach's sight began to fail. He suffered a rather gory operation which was unsuccessful and cost him what little sight remained.

Bach at the organ.
A court orchestra with Frederick the Great playing the flute.

The Bach family crest

Bach never left Germany, so he didn't become famous during his lifetime like Handel, who travelled widely. In fact, after his death, most of his music was forgotten until, in the 19th century, it was once more brought to people's notice by Mendelssohn.

Bach's six Brandenburg Concertos are written in the style of the Italian *concerto grosso*. That is, the composer contrasts two groups of instruments — a small group of soloists called the *concertino*, and a larger group of strings called the *ripieno* (an Italian word meaning 'full'). Sometimes the *concertino* instruments play on their own; sometimes they are heard in combination with the ripieno group.

There is also what is known as a *continuo* part which is played by a harpsichord and a low string instrument, usually a cello. As you can see from Bach's own manuscript on the right, the composer writes only a bass line for the *continuo*. Above this, the harpsichord player is expected to invent chords, to fill out the harmonies when the *ripieno* group is playing, and to play supporting harmonies when the *concertino* instruments are playing on their own.

Each of Bach's six *Brandenburg Concertos* is for a different combination of instruments. In the second concerto, the *concertino* group is made up of a trumpet, a flute, an oboe, and a violin.

BACH'S OWN MANUSCRIPT OF THE END OF THE THIRD MOVEMENT

First movement: Allegro (lively — and fairly fast)

The main theme (A) is played by both *concertino* and *ripieno* groups:
Between appearances of this theme, we hear another for the soloists to play in turn, supported by the *continuo* (B). First we hear the violin. Then (after the main theme) the oboe, while the violin plays an accompaniment; then the flute, with the accompaniment played by the oboe; finally the trumpet with flute accompaniment.

Try to get to know these two themes, and listen for them. Notice how Bach varies the combination of sounds, always keeping up the lively rhythm.

Second movement: Andante (at a walking pace)

Only three of the *concertino* group are used — flute, oboe and violin — supported by the *continuo*. The trumpet and the *ripieno* group are silent. There is a single theme (C), heard in *imitation* — one instrument plays the theme, then another 'imitates' it.
Sometimes Bach weaves his music around the first part of the theme (a); sometimes he used the second part (b). The peaceful mood of this flowing movement contrasts well with the brilliance and gaiety of the outer movements.

Third movement: Allegro assai (very lively)

The third movement is short and joyously rhythmic. After being silent in the slow movement, the trumpet announces the theme, which is perfectly suited to its brilliant sound (D). The other soloists are heard in turn: oboe, violin, then flute. The music is then built round this theme which is passed from one instrument to another. Listen towards the end for the theme played in the bass.

Joseph Haydn AUSTRIA 1732-1809

Andante and Allegro from Trumpet Concerto in E flat

Haydn's father, who was a wheelwright, soon discovered that his son had a good singing voice. He sent him to Vienna, where he received a sound musical training as a cathedral choir-boy.

At that time, each rich nobleman had his own orchestra. After a few years' service as a valet, Haydn became a violinist in the court orchestra of Prince Esterházy of Hungary. Later he became conductor of the orchestra *(Kapellmeister)*, a post he held for nearly thirty years. As Kapellmeister, he was expected to write music for the Prince's chapel and orchestra, and to rehearse the musicians.

Haydn playing in a string quartet.

Joseph Haydn

The trumpet

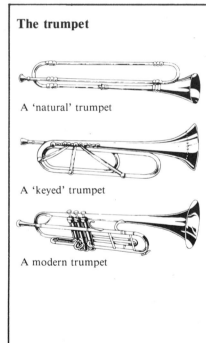

A 'natural' trumpet

A 'keyed' trumpet

A modern trumpet

The 'natural' trumpet which was used until the time of Haydn could only play certain notes, rather like a bugle. To get the lower notes, the player slackened his lips as he blew into the mouthpiece; to get the higher notes, he tightened his lips. If a composer wrote a *tune* for the 'natural' trumpet, he had to use the higher notes since there was a greater range of notes in the high register than in the low one. This is why the trumpet part of Bach's second Brandenburg Concerto is so high. Haydn wrote his Trumpet Concerto for a player who invented a trumpet with keys, rather like those of a saxophone. This meant the instrument could play low notes lying close together, making a greater range of notes available. (See theme B, facing page). Unfortunately, boring the holes for the keys in the side of the instrument caused a weakening of the tone quality, and so the 'keyed' trumpet never came into general use. Around 1830, however, the 'modern' trumpet with three valves was introduced. When a player presses a valve he is actually increasing the length of the tube, so that a new set of notes is made available. So by using the valves, and also altering his lip-pressure, he can play any note he chooses.

Announcement of a concert in Vienna in 1796 in which both Haydn and Beethoven took part. Haydn conducted 'new compositions', and 'Il Signore Bethofen', who was then 26, played a piano concerto.

The concerto

Each of Bach's Brandenburg Concertos was written for a *group* of soloists. In the second half of the 18th century, however, it became more usual to write a concerto for one soloist. Generally a solo concerto was written in three 'movements'. Sometimes a concerto was written with a particular player in mind, so that the composer was able to write passages to suit that soloist. In fact, there was usually a place towards the end of a movement when the orchestra was silent while the soloist showed off his technique with some dazzling playing. This kind of passage is called a *cadenza*.

The visiting card which Haydn gave to friends when he had reached old age: 'All my strength is gone; I am old and weak.'

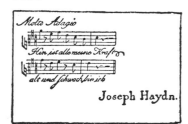

Andante (at a walking pace)

This movement is quite short, and is in three sections. The solo trumpet is accompanied by a flute, 2 oboes, bassoon and strings. The lilting main theme (A) is played first by the orchestra, and then repeated exactly by the trumpet. *(Cantabile* means 'in a singing style').

The 'middle section' immediately follows (B) changing the key from A flat major to the rather unusual key of C flat major — a change of key which would have been quite impossible for the 'natural' trumpet, but causing no difficulty for the keyed trumpet for which Haydn wrote this concerto.

When the main theme (A) returns, Haydn gives it straight away to the solo trumpet. There is a short *coda* (or ending) reminding us of theme B.

Allegro (lively — and fairly fast)

There are two important themes in this movement. Both are played by the orchestra before the soloist begins. First we hear the main theme (C) played by the strings, then repeated by the full orchestra.

The second theme (D) immediately follows. Then we hear both themes played by the trumpet.

Haydn designed this movement as a *rondo*—which means that one main theme (in this case, theme C) keeps 'coming round', with other contrasting material heard in between. Listen for each appearance of the main theme in this *rondo*. How many times does it come round?

Wolfgang Amadeus Mozart AUSTRIA 1756-1791

Third Movement from Horn Concerto No. 3 in E flat

The horn

Years ago the horn was exactly what its name suggests — the horn of an animal. In the 17th and 18th centuries, people used horns for hunting. The hunting horn at this time was a long piece of tubing, coiled into a circle, with a mouth-piece at one end and a wide *bell* at the other. The 'natural' horn, for which Mozart wrote his four Horn Concertos, was a smaller version of the hunting-horn.

Like the natural trumpet, the natural horn could only play those notes available from a single length of tubing. Actually horn-players found that pushing their hand into the bell would raise or lower the pitch of a note, so that a few more notes could be obtained. Then a better way of getting a wider range of notes was invented. An extra bit of tubing called a *crook* was inserted, so increasing the overall length of the instrument. This made possible a whole new series of notes. A horn-player usually had a set of nine crooks of different sizes. At the beginning of a piece a composer might write notes available from one length of tubing, then later in the piece write notes available from another. But he had to give the player a few bars rest in order to change crooks.

An 18th century French hunting horn.

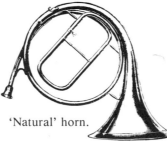

'Natural' horn.

Modern
French horn.

The young Mozart at the piano with his father and sister.

Around 1820, the 'modern' horn with three valves came into use. It is often called the *French horn*, possibly because of its early use in France. The valves do the work of the old-fashioned crooks — they add in extra bits of tubing. So by using the valves, and altering the pressure of his lips, a horn-player can play a complete range of notes.

The player supports the instrument by lightly resting his hand inside the bell. The tone of the horn is usually round and mellow, but if the player pushes his hand well inside the bell and blows very hard it can sound very brassy. A pear-shaped *mute* can be inserted into the bell, making the tone sound muffled and distant. There are usually 4 horns in an orchestra.

Mozart and his sister, Nannerl, were taught to play the harpsichord at a very early age by their father, Leopold. At the age of five, Mozart was already composing short pieces as well. A year later, Leopold took his gifted children on a four-year tour of Europe. Mozart even played for Empress Maria Theresa in Vienna at the age of seven. The story goes that, after playing for her, Mozart climbed onto her lap and kissed her!

To all Lovers of Sciences.

THE greatest Prodigy that Europe, or that even Human Nature has to boast of, is, without Contradiction, the little German Boy WOLFGANG MOZART, a Boy, Eight Years old, who has, and indeed very justly, raised the Admiration not only of the greatest Men, but also of the greatest Musicians in Europe. It is hard to say, whether his Execution upon the Harpsichord and his playing and singing at Sight, or his own Caprice, Fancy, and Compositions for all Instruments, are most astonishing. The Father of this Miracle, being obliged by Desire of several Ladies and Gentlemen to postpone, for a very short Time, his Departure from England, will give an Opportunity to hear this little Composer and his Sister, whose musical Knowledge wants not Apology. Performs every Day in the Week, from Twelve to Three o'Clock in the Great Room, at the Swan and Hoop, Cornhill. Admittance 2s. 6d. each Person.

The two Children will play also together with four Hands upon the same Harpsichord, and put upon it a Handkerchief, without seeing the Keys.

Announcement from a London newspaper, 1765

The Mozart family, from the Mozart Museum in Salzburg.

Mozart wrote his four Horn Concertos for a talented player called Leutgeb, who kept a cheese-shop in Vienna.

Mozart enjoyed a joke. The manuscripts of the Horn Concertos are covered with all kinds of joking remarks directed at Leutgeb. The second concerto has the dedication: 'Wolfgang Amadé Mozart sich über den Leutgeb Esel, Ochs und Naar, erbarmt zu Wien den 27 Mai 1783' (Wolfgang Amadeus Mozart has taken pity on Leutgeb, ass, ox and fool, Vienna 27th May 1783). Other remarks are scattered throughout the score, such as: 'go it Signor Asino.'; 'take a little breath'; 'poor swine!'; and 'thank God, here's the end!' There were other jokes, too. Mozart wrote the fourth concerto in four different inks — red, green, blue and black — just to confuse the poor hornplayer. And a *fast* movement was marked *adagio* (slowly). Perhaps Leutgeb tended to drag in quick movements. Even so, composer and player were probably the best of friends.

Points to listen for
This movement is a *rondo* —the main theme keeps 'coming round', with contrasting themes heard in between.
1. The main theme (A), first played by the horn, then by the orchestra. The horn joins in again towards the end.
2. The first contrasting theme (B). Later, listen for hunting-like fanfares from the horn and other instruments.
3. Theme A comes round again.
4. The second contrasting theme (C). Each phrase is begun by the horn, then completed by the strings. A linking passage with more horn fanfares follows.
5. Then Theme A comes round for the last time.
6. A *coda* ends the movement.

Piano Concerto No. 2 in C minor

Not only was Rachmaninov a great composer and famous conductor, but also one of the most brilliant pianists the world has known. By the time he was nine years old he was so promising that he entered the Music Academy at St. Petersburg (now called Leningrad). When he was twelve, he went on to the Moscow Academy, arriving with 100 roubles from his grandmother sewn into a little bag round his neck.

One day he had to take a piano examination, and Tchaikovsky was one of the examiners. The highest score a student could get was 5. Rachmaninov chose to play one of his own pieces. When he had finished, Tchaikovsky walked across to the table and wrote '5' on the mark-sheet. He thought for a moment, then added three plus signs. Turning to the young student, he said 'That wasn't an examination — that was a concert!' From then on the two became firm friends.

When he left the Academy Rachmaninov began to build up a reputation as a composer as well as a pianist. He wrote songs, piano pieces and a piano concerto; he also wrote a symphony which was not a great success. Its failure, together with news of Tchaikovsky's death, depressed Rachmaninov so much that for months he was unable to compose at all. But he still continued to thrill audiences with his dazzling piano-playing. One of his pieces, the Prelude in C sharp minor, became very popular. In fact he was asked to play it so often that he grew to dislike it.

Then, in 1900, when Rachmaninov was thinking of writing another piano concerto, he met a hypnotist called Dr. Nikolai Dahl. Rachmaninov visited him frequently. On each visit, the Doctor would relax him, then in a quiet voice repeat over and over: 'You will begin to work on your concerto . . . You will work with great ease . . . The music will be of excellent quality . . .'

Later, Rachmaninov said: 'Although it may sound incredible, this treatment really helped me. New musical ideas began to stir within me — far more than I needed for a concerto . . .'

When the work was finished, Rachmaninov dedicated it to Dr. Dahl. With its dramatic contrasts between piano and orchestra, and big sweeping melodies, reminding us of the music of Tchaikovsky whom Rachmaninov so greatly admired, the concerto was an immediate success.

During his lifetime, Rachmaninov travelled widely, conducting concerts and playing the piano wherever he went. To his regret, he found he had less and less time in which to compose. When the Russian Revolution broke out in 1917, he left Russia never again to return. He settled in America, and died in California in 1943.

Points to listen for

First movement: *Moderato* (at a moderate pace)

1. The piano begins, alone, with 9 dramatic chords, growing in intensity, and ranging from *pianissimo* to *fortissimo*.

2. Then the soloist begins a swirling accompaniment while the orchestra plays the first theme (A): a passionate, sweeping melody lasting 45 bars. The piano repeats the second half of this long theme.

3. The second theme (B), full of sadness and yearning, is given to the piano with occasional support from the orchestra. The soloist repeats it an octave higher, decorating it with running-notes.

4. In the *development section* (where these themes are 'developed', or worked out) a rhythmic figure (C) becomes very important, and is heard in combination with parts of themes A and B. It comes from part of theme B itself (marked 'x'). The music builds to a climax, then:

5. Theme A returns in the orchestra, *fortissimo*, and as a march, while C is played by the piano in huge, pounding chords. When theme B returns, it is played by a horn rather slowly. The piano reflects dreamily on theme C, then the pace quickens as a *coda* ends the movements.

Second movement: *Adagio sostenuto* (slow and sustained)

Various orchestral instruments are chosen by Rachmaninov to play solo melodies. Notice how he shares the interest, and the accompaniment, between piano and orchestra.

1. Muted strings set the peaceful mood, changing key from C minor (the key of the first movement) to E major. Then the piano begins a flowing accompaniment above which will float the main theme (D) on flute and clarinet.

2. The piano plays the theme, very simply, while the orchestra accompanies.

3. A lengthy section, with two climaxes, based on figure 'y' of theme D.

4. A flourish on the piano introduces a contrasting section at a quicker pace, ending with a *cadenza* (a section where the orchestra remains silent while the soloist shows off his technique with some dazzling playing).

5. The quiet, peaceful mood returns — theme D played on muted violins, the piano accompanying as it did at the beginning of the movement.

6. Then the music is lifted up as it broadens into a rich *coda* — big, rocking chords from the piano against long-drawn phrases on the violins.

Third movement: *Allegro scherzando* (lively and playful)

1. A march-like orchestral introduction returns us from E major to C minor.

2. A glittering *cadenza* for the soloist leads into the first theme (E).

3. The lyrical second theme (F) is given to violas, then repeated by the piano.

4. A rather mysterious passage follows: cymbals lightly brushed together and *staccato* orchestral chords, against running-notes on the piano.

5. The *development section* — in which theme E is worked out in various ways.

6. Theme F — first on flute and violins, then piano — followed again by the mysterious passage with brushed cymbals.

7. Gradually, a climax is built up — very much in the style of Tchaikovsky.

8. Then another *cadenza* for the soloist leads to:

9. The final appearance of theme F, played triumphantly in C major by the orchestra while the soloist accompanies with massive, rich chords.

10. Then a brilliant *coda* to round off the whole work.

Georges Bizet FRANCE 1838-1875

Incidental music to 'L'Arlésienne'

Incidental music to a play is music specially composed to be heard at certain times during the performance. It might introduce an act or scene, or be played between scenes to keep the audience's interest while the scenery is changed, or even serve as background music while the characters are speaking. In 1872, the Vaudeville Theatre in Paris decided to stage a play by Alphonse Daudet called *L'Arlésienne* ('The Girl from Arles'). The French composer Bizet — later to become famous for his colourful opera *Carmen* — was invited to compose incidental music for the play. Bizet was then 34, and was to live for only three more years.

Arles is a town in Provence, and Bizet thought it a good idea to use two Provençal folk tunes to give his music local colour. He chose a Provençal carol called 'Marcho dei Rei' (March of the Kings) and a Provençal dance tune called 'Danse dei Chivaux-Frus'.

The 'Bridge at Arles',
by Van Gogh.

Bizet in 1860.

Bizet's music exactly matches the mood of *L'Arlésienne*. The play is set on a farm and is about two brothers. One, called 'the Innocent', is rather slow-witted. The second brother, Fréderi, has fallen passionately in love with a girl from the nearby town of Arles. Although the play takes its title from this character, and events are centred around her, she never actually appears on stage.

Shortly after Fréderi's parents have agreed to his marriage with the girl, they discover that she has had several lovers already and deceived them all in turn. The latest one arrives at the farm with love letters which she has sent to him. This is Mitifio, a fierce horseman of the district of Provence known as the Camargue.

Completely broken by this discovery, Fréderi begins to lose his reason. In despair, he hurls himself to his death from the highest roof of the farm buildings while his mother watches helplessly from the courtyard.

Neither the play nor the music was a success at the first performance. But later Bizet arranged four of the pieces as a *suite* (or 'group' of pieces) and then the music became very popular.

Prelude

This is played before the curtain rises and sets the mood of the whole play. It is in three sections.

First, variations on the Provençal carol 'March of the Kings' (A). We hear the tune five times. Notice how Bizet makes it sound interesting each time without altering the actual melody:

1. Strings, woodwind and horns play the theme *fortissimo* and in unison (that is, no chords or harmonies but with everyone playing the same notes).

2. The melody is played quietly by the clarinet with rich, flowing harmonies for flute, cor anglais and 2 bassoons.

3. Woodwind and horns play the melody in unison against an agitated accompaniment for strings, also in unison. Notice the exciting beat on the snare-drum, and the gradual *crescendos,* each one followed by a sudden drop to *pianissimo.*

4. The melody is played *legato* (smoothly) by cellos in the major key, with a horn counter-melody. There is a contrasting accompaniment shared between the 2 bassoons played *staccato* (crisp and detached).

5. Full orchestra, *fortissimo,* and with a definite march rhythm. A quiet ending.

The second section of the Prelude contains a melody for saxophone (B) which represents the slow-witted brother called 'the Innocent'. Bizet was the first great composer to use the saxophone.

The final section consists of a despairing theme for strings with a throbbing accompaniment, representing Fréderi's ill-fated love for the Girl from Arles. There is a passionate climax, marked *fff;* then a quiet close.

Minuet

This is played between Acts 3 and 4 of the play. The music is in three main sections: (A B A) known as *Minuet* and *Trio*. A is the main *minuet,* originally a stately court dance with 3 beats to each bar. B is a contrasting section called the *trio,* so called because it used to be written for three musical instruments. After the *trio*, the first *minuet* is played again without repeats. Over the years, minuets had become faster. Bizet marks his to be played *allegro giocoso* — lively and jokingly.

1. *Minuet,* itself in two sections. The first section (theme D) is played loudly by the strings. These 8 bars are repeated.

2. The second section begins with woodwind, brass and kettle-drums, answered by unison strings (E). Then a quieter passage for flutes. This section is also repeated.

3. The *trio* begins with a bagpipe-like *drone*—2 notes repeated a fifth apart. Clarinet and saxophone play a flowing theme (F) while violins weave a counter-melody. Later, violins and cellos have the main theme, with the counter-melody now given to woodwind and harp.

4. More work for the flutes, chattering away in thirds above *pizzicato* strings.

5. Theme F again, violins and cellos.

6. A linking passage, first oboe then violins, and the *minuet* returns, now shortened a great deal and played more softly.

Adagietto (G)

There is a rather touching sub-plot in the play, about an old farmer's wife, Mère Renaud, and an ageing shepherd called Balthazar. They were sweethearts in their youth, and in the play they meet again for the first time in fifty years. The tenderly expressive *Adagietto* is played as background music during the scene where they meet. It is scored for strings only, without double basses. On the right you can see the complete score of this short piece. *Bratsche* means 'viola'; all the strings are asked to play *con sordini* (with mutes), giving a soft veiled quality to the tone. Even so, notice the wide range of expression called for: from *pianissimo* at the beginning, eventually to *forte* (bar 23) a *crescendo* to *fortissimo* (bar 25), and then a sudden *diminuendo* (getting softer) to *pianissimo* once more. *Smorzando*, at the end, means 'fading to nothing'. Bizet marks the music to be played *adagio* (slowly). By giving it the title *Adagietto*, he means 'a short piece at a slow pace'.

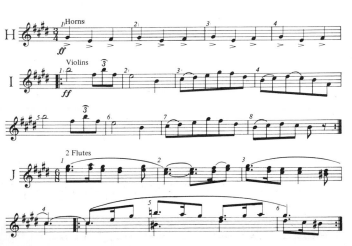

Carillon (H, I, J)

This is the prelude to Act 4 of *L'Arlésienne* which opens with merry-making to celebrate the festival of Saint Eloi. But Bizet both lengthened and re-orchestrated the piece when he arranged it to make a conclusion to his *suite*. A *carillon* is a set of church bells worked not by pulling on rope but mechanically by means of a keyboard and pedals.

1. The joyful ringing of the village church bells is represented by a repeated three-note figure played by horns, harp, 2nd violins and violas (H). The violas are played here with short repeated strokes of the bow; the 2nd violins play the figure *pizzicato*. A scrap of tune played over and over like this is called an *ostinato* (Italian for 'obstinate'). During the piece the horns play it 98 times.

2. Against the *ostinato* we hear the merry-making of the villagers (I).

3. The *ostinato* stops for a gently-flowing theme on 2 flutes (J), accompanied softly by 8 violins and 4 violas. This is really from another part of the play, the entrance of old Mère Renaud. Bizet uses it here as a contrast to the brilliant music of the merry-making.

4. 2 oboes join the flutes, and the accompaniment is doubled to 16 violins and 8 violas.

5. Then the other strings join in, the violins taking the melody.

6. Listen for the *ostinato* to steal in on the horns, linking to the return of theme I.

7. Theme I again — first played by an oboe, then by violins as before — but always with the *ostinato* in the background.

Farandole

Bizet's suite from his incidental music to *L'Arlésienne* became so popular that after his death his friend Guiraud arranged a second suite. As a brilliant conclusion to *his* suite, Guiraud cleverly builds up an exciting piece based on the Provençal folk tunes which Bizet had used ('Marcho dei Rei' and 'Danse dei Chivaux-Frus'). Guiraud calls the piece *Farandole*. Here is how the music is put together.

1. First half of the march (theme **A**, page 51) grandly played by the full orchestra.

2. First half of the march in *canon* —one group of instruments starts to play the tune, then another group joins in later with the same tune (rather like a *round*, such as 'Frère Jacques'). Example K shows how it is done.

3. A soft beat on the tabor, and flute and clarinet begin the dance (L).

4. The shrill-voiced piccolo joins in the second half of the tune, with sharp little rushes played off-the-beat by violins. Other instruments gradually join in.

5. First half of the march, played by woodwind and strings in unison.

6. A brief snatch of the dance-tune — flute, then piccolo.

7. Second half of the march — first phrase in unison; second richly harmonised.

8. Again, the dance-tune — with more instruments joining in to build a climax.

9. Then, excitingly, the march and the dance-tune played together. The march is played by the brass while woodwind and strings take the dance. The first half of the tune is repeated with bass drum and cymbals added, the entire orchestra asked to play *ffff*! A brilliant, breathless conclusion, the excitement heightened by swift cymbal-clashes.

Edvard Grieg NORWAY 1843-1907

Incidental music to Peer Gynt

In 1874 the Norwegian playwright, Henrik Ibsen, prepared a stage version of his dramatic poem, *Peer Gynt*, based upon the exploits of a real character who lived in Norway at the end of the 18th century. He asked his fellow-countryman, Edvard Grieg, to compose some incidental music. Grieg accepted but, though he admired Ibsen's play, the task proved more difficult than he had expected. At the end of the summer, he wrote:

'*Peer Gynt* is progressing very slowly, and there is no question of it being ready by the autumn. It is the most unmusical of subjects — with a few exceptions such as Solveig's songs, all of which I have finished. And I have done some of "The Hall of the Mountain King", which I really cannot bear listening to . . . ' Even though Grieg's music does not always match the bitterness of certain parts of *Peer Gynt*, it is marvellous music for all that.

Peer Gynt is a selfish, headstrong, yet likeable character, always trying to impress by boasting about his adventures. Arriving uninvited at a wedding, he carries off the bride, Ingrid, but soon tires of her and leaves her on a mountain side. Now a hunted outlaw, Peer finds his way deep into the caves beneath the mountains — the underground kingdom of the goblin-like Trolls and their evil ruler, the Mountain King. At first they welcome him, but he is rude about their music and dancing, and in a fury they attack him. He manages to escape and builds a hut, high up on the mountainside. The gentle Solveig, a village girl who loves Peer, leaves family and friends to join him. But Peer deserts her too. He risks capture to visit his mother, Åse, who is ill. She dies while he is with her. Peer decides to travel, seeking wealth and adventure in North Africa. Years pass, yet still he cannot find true happiness. In the end he returns to Norway, after a voyage of storm and shipwreck. He meets a mysterious Button-Moulder — the Devil in disguise — who tells him he must die unless he can find someone who really wants him to live. Peer knows that he is not fit for Heaven, but is horrified to find that his sins have not been serious enough for Hell. His soul must be melted down as mere waste. The idea of complete destruction is unbearable — he would rather survive, even in Hell! Figures and phantoms emerge from the past to accuse him, then vanish. He is about to leave with the Button-Moulder when he sees a hut, now forgotten on the mountain side. Solveig, now old and almost blind, hears his voice and slowly comes out of the hut. 'Is there no place for me — on earth, in Heaven, nor in Hell?' he cries, 'Yes,' comes the gentle answer which finally saves him. 'Here — in my heart.'

Morning

A piece originally intended to introduce a scene set in the Sahara Desert, beginning with a sunrise. Later it was used to open Act IV when the sun is setting on the North African Coast! However, the music fits perfectly the title which Grieg has given it, but rather as if he were thinking of the dewy freshness of a clear Norwegian morning with sunrise over pinewoods, mountains and fjords. A lilting melody, on flute and oboe alternately (A), is followed by the warmth of strings as the rising sun bathes the landscape in glowing colours. Listen carefully to the opening, and compare the clear tone of the flute with the rather reedier sound of the oboe.

Later there are smooth phrases for the cellos.

Example B shows how the music ends. Listen for the melody to be played by a horn. Woodwind decorations seem to suggest birdsongs.

Death of Åse

Åse's hut. Evening. The room is lit by a wood fire; the cat is on the chair. Peer risks capture as an outlaw to visit his mother, Åse, who is ill. They talk of happier times and Peer plays a game he enjoyed as a child, pretending the bed is a sleigh crossing snow and ice. He is still lost in this fantasy as his mother dies:

'Mother, why do you stare at me? It's me — Peer — your son.'
(He feels her hands and forehead, then slowly closes her eyes.)
'There, you can sleep now. Your long journey's over . . .
Thanks for the care you've shown me, the lullabies you've
sung me — and the beatings. Now, *you* must thank me.'
(He touches her lips with his cheek.)
(Softly) 'That . . . was the driver's tip . . .'

The music is slow, and scored for strings alone — muted (except double basses) to give a soft, muffled tone. Theme C is played 3 times, higher each time, and growing louder to a climax. Then the music sinks gradually lower and softer, fading away as Åse dies.

The bassoon

This is the lowest-sounding of the four main woodwind instruments: flute, oboe, clarinet and bassoon. The Italian name is *fagotto*, meaning 'bundle' — perhaps because the bassoon looks rather like a bundle of sticks. Because the total length of the tube that makes up the bassoon is more than 8 feet long, it is doubled on itself to make it more manageable. Even then the player has to support it by a sling. The bassoon has a double reed—rather like the oboe's, but broader—which fits into the end of a curved metal tube called the *crook*.

In the lower register the tone sounds dry, even comic. The higher notes can sound smooth and plaintive.

The oboe

This woodwind instrument has a *double reed*. The player blows between the two reeds, forcing them to vibrate against each other so that they, in turn, cause the air inside the instrument to vibrate. The oboe is good for slow, melancholy melodies but can sound gay and perky when given fast, rhythmic tunes.

Anitra's dance

Anitra is the daughter of a Bedouin Chief whom Peer meets during his adventures in North Africa. She dances for him, but then robs him of all his wealth and leaves him stranded in the desert.

Grieg uses a small number of instruments but very effectively; muted strings for the melody (D); pizzicato strings for the rhythmic accompaniment; and a triangle to add an Eastern flavour. There is a smoother contrasting theme for violins in thirds (E), after which the instruments seem to chase each other.

In the Hall of the Mountain King

Deep in the caves beneath the mountains. Evil and ugly trolls stealthily emerge from the shadows and surround Peer. Faster and faster they dance round him, pinching and scratching him until he is terrified.

Troll Courtiers:	What shall we do to him?
A Young Troll:	Let me wrench off his fingers!
Another:	Let me chew off his lips!
A Troll Maiden:	I'll tear out his hair!
Another:	I'll suck out his eyes!
A Troll Witch with a ladle:	Shall we boil him to a broth?
Another Witch with an axe:	Or spit him and roast him?

(With blood-curdling shrieks they surround Peer.)

There is a single theme, repeated 18 times. First we hear it on cellos and basses with bassoon accompaniment, then these instruments exchange parts (F). The dry tone of the bassoon is well suited to the awkward movements of the trolls. The music gets faster and louder as more instruments join in. In fact the whole piece is a gradual *crescendo*, rising in pitch and excitement from beginning to end.

Ingrid's lament

This music begins Act II. Having carried off Ingrid, the bride, Peer now abandons her on the mountainside.

After two passionate outbursts, each followed by brass calls and muffled drums, low violins begin Ingrid's despairing lament (G).

The lament is repeated an octave higher. Then kettle-drums menacingly beat out an insistent rhythm, while the strings sink lower and lower. Then the music ends as it began.

Arabian dance

Arab girls entertain Peer in the desert at the beginning of the scene from which Anitra's Dance is taken. Seeing Peer's fair skin, and stolen robes which he is wearing, they think he is their long-awaited Prophet.

The music is rhythmic, brash and colourful. Grieg gives it an Arabian flavour by including triangle, bass drum, tambourine and piccolo (H).

Return of Peer Gynt

Music to open the final Act: On board a ship in the North Sea off the Norwegian coast. It is sunset and the weather is stormy. Tired of his wanderings, Peer, now an old man, has decided to return to his native land.

We hear the pounding of waves and the screaming of wind in the rigging (I). Thunderous chords warn us that, later in the scene, the threatening storm will break and the ship will be wrecked.

Solveig's song

Solveig sits at the door of the hut on the mountainside, spinning in the sunshine. A short introduction for strings sets the gentle mood. Harp and lower strings strum an accompaniment to the wistful violin melody (J). We hear the whirring of the spinning wheel in the gently rhythmic refrain (K), echoing Solveig's confidence that, one day, Peer will return to her.

Both song and refrain are repeated an octave higher. Then a quiet close, similar to the music of the introduction.

Dr. Faustus and the Devil

Hector Berlioz

Rákóczy March

from The Damnation of Faust

There have been many stories and plays based on the Faust legend. Faust is a man who sells his soul to the Devil. The Devil promises him anything he asks for — youth, money, power — but when he dies, his soul will belong to the Devil.

Many writers have been fascinated by the Faust legend. Christopher Marlowe, an Elizabethan playwright and a friend of Shakespeare's, wrote a play called 'Dr. Faustus' in 1588. The 19th century German dramatist, Goethe, also made use of the story in one of his plays. But the two plays end differently: Marlow's Faust is damned for ever and carried off to Hell by the Devil; Goethe's Faust repents and is finally saved.

The French composer, Hector Berlioz, thought this legend was an ideal story to set to music.

He used the Faust legend on two occasions. In 1829, he composed 'Eight Scenes from Goethe's *Faust*'. Several years later, in 1846, he decided to write a larger work, using some of the first music but altering it a great deal. It was to be called *The Damnation of Faust*, a grand orchestral work, rather like an opera but intended to be performed in the concert hall without costumes or scenery.

Then, when Berlioz was in Vienna, someone — possibly the Hungarian composer Liszt — lent him a collection of Hungarian melodies, one of which was the Rákóczy March. He was so enthusiastic about this piece of music that he decided to set the first part of *The Damnation of Faust* in Hungary in order to make use of this march.

A Pact with the Devil

Here is part of a Pact between the Devil and a French nobleman in 1676:

1. Lucifer, you are bound to deliver to me immediately 100,000 pounds of money in gold!

2. You will deliver to me the first Tuesday of every month 1,000 pounds.

3. You will bring me this gold in current money, of such kind that not only I, but also all those to whom I may wish to give some, may use it.

4. The aforesaid gold must not be false, must not disappear in one's hand, or turn to stone or coals . . .

5. If I need a considerable sum of money, no matter when or for what purpose, you are bound to deliver to me secret or buried treasure . . .

The Polish composer, Chopin, once said: 'Berlioz's music sounds as if he merely splatters his pen across the music paper.'

In *The Damnation of Faust*, the March is heard as the Hungarian Army approaches from the distance and marches past the open window of Faust's study — which is why Berlioz begins the march *piano* but ends it *fortissimo*.

Cartoon of Berlioz conducting, by the French cartoonist Gustave Doré.

Berlioz was a conductor as well as a composer. He mixed and combined instruments in unusual ways never before attempted. He once described his ideal orchestra. It was to include 240 strings, 30 harps, 30 grand pianos, with woodwind, brass and percussion instruments in proportion. Of course, he never actually wrote a piece for such an orchestra. But on one occasion, the King of Prussia said that he had heard that Berlioz wrote for 500 performers. Berlioz replied 'Your Majesty has been misinformed. I sometimes write for 480.' Indeed, his *Requiem* requires a huge orchestra, hundreds of singers, and no less than four brass bands!

The first performance of *The Damnation of Faust* was a failure, but now it is frequently performed in the concert hall, and sometimes even staged as an opera.

A few months after the music was completed, Berlioz was in Budapest, the capital of Hungary, to conduct a concert. He had with him the music of the 'Rákóczy March' and decided to include it in the concert. The editor of a Budapest newspaper came to him in great excitement. Here, again in Berlioz's own words, is an account of the conversation, and of the concert itself:

" 'I have seen your score of the Rákóczy March,' said he to the editor.

'Well?'

'You've marked the tune *piano*, and we're used to hearing it *fortissimo*.'

'Yes, by the gypsy orchestra. But never fear, you shall have a *forte* such as you have never heard before in your life!'

'Nevertheless, on the evening of the concert, I felt a tightening of the throat when the moment came to conduct the march. After a trumpet phrase, the tune appears, you will remember, performed *piano* by the flutes and clarinets, and accompanied *pizzicato* by the strings (Theme **A**). To this unexpected treatment the audience listened in silence. But when, after a long *crescendo*, fragments of the tune appeared, interrupted by dull beats on the bass drum (**C**) the concert hall began to seethe with an indescribable sound, and when at length the orchestra hurled forth the long-delayed *fortissimo*, the hall was shaken by the most unheard-of cries and stampings that shivered me with terror. I felt as if my hair was standing on end.' "

The Hungarian audience was so excited by Berlioz's orchestration of their national melody, that the piece had to be repeated.

(There is a second, contrasting, theme (**B**) which Berlioz does not mention above.)

Music for films

Recording the music for a film.

Here are some of the ways in which good film music can add to our enjoyment and understanding of a film:

1. It can conjure up a *mood* or *atmosphere*, often quicker and more effectively than words or pictures.

2. It can give us *information* by setting the atmosphere of a certain country, place, period of time.

3. It can *build up suspense* during an exciting scene; or prepare us for something *about to happen*, perhaps not hinted at by the pictures we see.

4. It can *emphasise an emotion* so that we feel it more strongly, such as pity, fear, sadness, laughter.

5. It can tell us something about a *character,* perhaps his state of mind, which the words and pictures might not make clear.

```
        TIMING SHEET          "SHADOW OF FEAR"
                                   72 X 6N

Time

000      Brand silhouetted in open doorway
001⅔     Snaps on torch; scans room
003      C.U. of eyes, moving left to right
005⅓     Camera pans around room, following torch-beam
009⅔     Beam rests on safe near window
010⅔     Brand approaches safe, camera tracking alongside
015⅓     C.S. of gloved hand appearing between curtains
016      Curtains suddenly wrenched apart!
```

Music has always played a very important part in the cinema. In the early days, silent films were accompanied by 'live' music, usually played on a piano or organ. The musician's job was to keep an eye on the screen and provide non-stop entertainment, changing the mood as the film required. Certain pieces of music became well-known to cinema-goers — a tearful melody called *Hearts and Flowers* for a sad scene, an urgent tune called *The Devil's Galop* for a chase, and so on.

Then in the late 1920's, the 'sound-track' was invented. The voices of the actors — and the background music — could be recorded onto the film itself and reproduced whenever it was shown. The days of the cinema pianist were over.

Writing music for a film is a demanding but rewarding task. The composer is first called in to see a 'rough cut'. This is the film, roughly assembled, but with the precise lengths of shots not yet finally decided. Both composer and director discuss which kind of music is needed, and at which points of the film it is to be heard.

Next, the film is edited, so that some sequences may be altered or shortened. Then a 'fine cut' is assembled — the film as it will be seen in the cinema. The composer is then given 'cue-sheets', or 'timing sheets', with very precise timings in seconds and in fractions of seconds. You will see from the cue-sheet (left) that the fractions are in thirds of a second. 35 millimetre film gives 16 'frames' to a foot. As it is shown at 24 frames a second, a foot of film lasts exactly two-thirds of a second.

The timings on the cue-sheets show the composer how he must plan his music, which must fit the film *exactly*. In the sequence shown on the left, a man enters a darkened room. At $16\frac{2}{3}$ seconds, someone is to leap from behind the curtains. If the composer writes his 'suspense' music in 4/4 time, at 90 crotchets to a minute, he knows that every crotchet will take $\frac{2}{3}$ of a second. A terrifying, crashing discord can then occur on the second beat of the seventh bar.

When the music is completed, the orchestra is called into the studio. The film is projected, without sound-track, onto a screen behind the players. The conductor has a very difficult job to do. Besides interpreting the music, he must keep his eye on the screen so that the music is recorded in precise synchronisation with the film.

Title-music: "The Big Country"   (Neff-Lewis Moross)

Besides making sure his music is precisely timed to fit the action, a composer must also write music which exactly matches the *mood* or *atmosphere* of each situation. The first impression he makes on his audience is, of course, with the opening title-music, which sets the mood of the whole film. Three composers worked as a team to write music for *The Big Country*. Immediately, an exciting 'cowboy' atmosphere is created: brass chords against a figure on high violins which suggests a lively American square-dance. Then the music swings into the main theme (A) above striding chords. It is repeated with a rhythm on the snare drum. Between appearances of the main theme we hear contrasting material for wind instruments with sparkling notes from the glockenspiel (B). The *coda*, or ending, brings back the opening square-dance idea.

The Funeral Scene from "Dr Zhivago"   (Maurice Jarre)

To record the music for this film took ten days. Besides an orchestra of 110 players there were other 'special' instruments, including zither, harpsichord, electric piano, organ, a six-foot gong, and 24 *balalaikas* (Russian plucked instruments, rather like triangular guitars). When writing music for this scene, Jarre faced several challenges. Most important were *timing,* and *atmosphere*. The whole film is a 'flash-back'; this scene shows Zhivago as a boy at his mother's funeral. The atmosphere is effectively set by flute and male voices — humming so low, they sound like groans. A female voice sings a lament with balalaikas adding their distinctive Russian colouring as the wind causes late leaves to flutter down from the almost-bare trees. We see the boy's face as he stares at his mother's body lying in the open coffin. Then, with terrifying finality, a huge percussive chord is timed precisely as the coffin-lid slams down. Three more thunderous chords as, in turn, the clasps are secured. The music mirrors the boy's thoughts and feelings more effectively than any spoken words . . .

Title-music: "The Guns of Navarone" (Dimitri Tiomkin)

This film was based upon a story by the popular writer, Alistair MacLean. The title-music sets the mood of daring and courage in the face of danger. After a challenge from the whole orchestra, horns play the main theme (C) — a catchy, rhythmic tune, superbly orchestrated. Instead of a contrasting theme, Tiomkin presents us with the main theme again, but now in the *minor* key, and with much lighter scoring (woodwind and glockenspiel).

Quiz 3

(Only 'cheat' — by looking back for an answer — if you really have to!)

1. Who composed . . . ?

Can you identify these themes? Give the title of each, together with the composer and his country.

a)

b)

c)

d)

e)

f)

g)

h)

i)

j)

2. Opposites

Arrange these words in pairs, each word with its 'opposite'. Then give the meaning of each one.

staccato	coda	fortissimo
pianissimo	allegro	ripieno
crescendo	legato	introduction
concertino	adagio	diminuendo

3. A legend in music

This is the (1—————) of a beautiful princess called (2———————), who lived in (3—————— —————————) at (4—————————————————). She was walking in the forest at (5————), one (6—————————) in (7————————), in the year (8————), when a wicked witch called (9————— —————), who lived in a (10——— —— ——————— —————) spied her, and whisked her away to a cave in (11——— —————————), where she was closely guarded by an evil (12—————).

Now fill in the gaps in the story by answering these questions:

1. A name given to a lengthy story from Scandinavia.
2. She danced for Peer Gynt.
3. One of Mussorgsky's *Pictures at an Exhibition*.
4. Bach wrote six concertos for the Margrave of . . .
5. One of Britten's *Sea Interludes*.
6. From Grieg's music to Ibsen's *Peer Gynt*.
7. When you are likely to hear Delius's bird.
8. An overture by Tchaikovsky.
9. One of Mussorgsky's 'Pictures' concerns this witch.
10. Her house, and her means of travelling!
11. An overture by Mendelssohn.
12. Another of Mussorgsky's 'Pictures'.

4. Musical Pairs

Arrange all these words into matching pairs:

forte	drum	double	French
grosso	Williams	bass	mouth
Ivanov	William	horn	organ
Tell	Ippolitov	kettle	Baba
Yaga	bassoon	Vaughan	barrel
piano	concerto	clarinet	piece

5. Musical Jigsaw

Clues Across

1. Low-pitched woodwind instrument.
6. Former name for Czechoslovakia.
7. Country where Debussy was born.
9. Wide end of a brass instrument.
11. The Hell of Finnish mythology.
12. Composer of *Peter Grimes*.
14. Another name for snare drum.
15. Nationality of Vaughan Williams.
16. Villa-Lobos's transport.
17. He had 20 children!
19. Author of the play *Peer Gynt*.
21. Peer Gynt's mother.
23. He wrote music for *Peer Gynt*.
24. Name given to trumpets and horns before valves were introduced.

Clues Down

2. Country whose national instruments are guitar and castanets.
3. Woodwind instrument with a double reed.

4. Sibelius's country.
5. Islands visited by Mendelssohn.
7. Woodwind instrument with no reed.
8. Delius's country.
9. Bach wrote six . . . Concertos.
10. He wrote music for *L' Arlésienne*.
13. 'Obstinate' phrase which repeats.
18. English and French varieties.
20. Second section of the Overture
    to *William Tell*.
22. Essential to all wind instruments.

6. Musical anagrams

The first letters of the answers, when rearranged, will give a composer's name.

A
  a) Composer of *William Tell*.
  b) Composer of *Procession of the Sardar*.
  c) Wagner's nationality.
  d) Composer of *Wedding Day at Troldhaugen*.
  e) Kind of horn?

B
  a) Composer of *Danse Macabre*.
  b) Music played between acts or scenes.
  c) Composer of *The Swan of Tuonela*.
  d) Nationality of composer of *William Tell*.
  e) Nationality of composer of *Peer Gynt*.
  f) *1812* and *The Hebrides* are examples of this kind of piece.
  g) Nationality of Rachmaninov.

The first letters here will give a country:

C
  a) A passage in a concerto where the soloist shows off his technique.
  b) Italian word meaning 'at a walking pace'.
  c) He orchestrated Mussorgsky's *Pictures at an Exhibition*.

d) The same composer's nationality.
e) Piece by Mussorgsky, orchestrated by Rimsky-Korsakov.
f) Nationality of the composer of *On Hearing the First Cuckoo in Spring*.

7. More anagrams

These are composers:

A
  a) RAMTOZ
  b) SHLOSENDNEM
  c) TEZBI
  d) ZIRELOB
  e) SOSKYGRUMS
  F) SANTAME
  g) TANSI SENAS

And these are Italian words directing how music should be played:

B
  a) SNOUT TOES
  b) REAL LOG
  c) ATE LOG
  d) SECOND REC
  e) TOCATACS
  f) DUMODINIEN
  g) OZICAPTIZ

8. Tally-O!

Many Italian words used in music end in 'o'. How many can you remember? Make a list, then add the English meanings. (At least 25 have been mentioned in this book).

9. Musical alphabet

1. Nationality of Mozart and Haydn.   A
2. French composer of a Hungarian march   B
3. Nationality of the composer of *Vltava*. C
4. Poem set to music by Saint-Saëns.   D
5. Another name for *cor anglais*.   E
6. Sibelius's nationality — complete!   F

7. 'Sliding' effect, as made by a trombone.   G
8. Keyboard instrument, plucked not hammered.   H
9. Music written specially for a play.   I
10. Christian name of the composer of *Finlandia*.   J
11. Name of the Finnish collection of legends.   K
12. Mozart's 'ox, ass and fool'.   L
13. Might quieten down the brass section.   M
14. Tone poem by Mussorgsky.   N
15. Usually begins an opera, perhaps a concert.   O
16. High pitched woodwind instrument.   P
17. Half a crotchet.   Q
18. Larger group of strings in a *Concerto Grosso*.   R
19. A group of pieces.   S
20. You can have it natural, keyed or with valves.   T
21. Pianos can be either 'grand', or . . .   U
22. Slightly larger than a violin.   V
23. Other players might take this cover when a percussionist plays this. (That's a crack!)   W
24. Another percussion instrument.   X
25. This Baba was a witch.   Y
26. A plucked string instrument from Austria.   Z

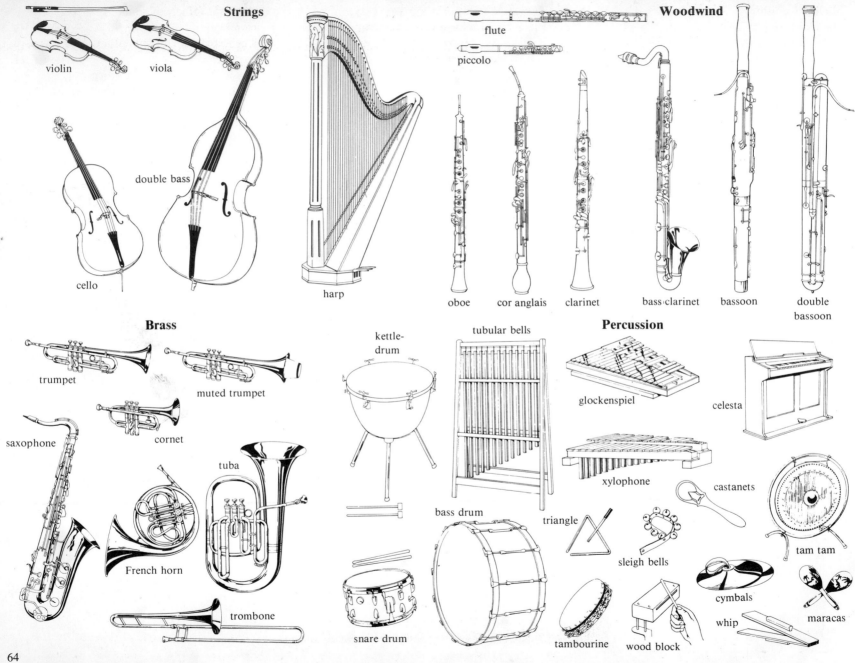

Strings

violin

viola

double bass

cello

harp

Woodwind

flute

piccolo

oboe

cor anglais

clarinet

bass clarinet

bassoon

double bassoon

Brass

trumpet

muted trumpet

cornet

saxophone

tuba

French horn

trombone

kettle-drum

tubular bells

Percussion

glockenspiel

celesta

xylophone

castanets

tam tam

bass drum

triangle

sleigh bells

cymbals

whip

maracas

snare drum

tambourine

wood block